TRACING YOUR MANCHESTER AND SALFORD ANCESTORS

i

FAMILY HISTORY FROM PEN & SWORD

TRACING YOUR MANCHESTER AND SALFORD ANCESTORS

A Guide for Family and Local Historians

Sue Wilkes

Pen & Sword
FAMILY HISTORY

For all my family

First published in Great Britain in 2017
PEN & SWORD FAMILY HISTORY
an imprint of
Pen & Sword Books Ltd
47 Church Street,
Barnsley South Yorkshire, S70 2AS

ISBN 978 1 47385 635 6

A CIP catalogue record for this book is
available from the British Library.

Typeset in Palatino and Optima by CHIC GRAPHICS

Printed and bound in England by
CPI Group (UK), Croydon, CR0 4YY

Pen & Sword Books Ltd incorporates the imprints of Pen & Sword
Archaeology, Atlas, Aviation, Battleground, Discovery, Family History,
History, Maritime, Military, Naval, Politics, Railways, Select, Social History,
Transport, True Crime, Claymore Press, Frontline Books, Leo Cooper,
Praetorian Press, Remember When, Seaforth Publishing and Wharncliffe.

For a complete list of Pen & Sword titles please contact
PEN & SWORD BOOKS LTD
47 Church Street, Barnsley, South Yorkshire, S70 2AS, England
E-mail: enquiries@pen-and-sword.co.uk
Website: www.pen-and-sword.co.uk

CONTENTS

Contents

ACKNOWLEDGEMENTS

As ever, I must express my gratitude to the many archivists and librarians who have patiently assisted with my enquiries, in particular David Govier of Manchester Libraries, Information and Archives, Duncan McCormick, Local History Librarian at Salford Local History Library, Marion Hewitt of the North West Film Archive, Michael Powell and Sue McLoughlin of Chetham's Library, and staff at Lancashire Archives. Thanks are also owed to the Library of Congress's Head of Reference Section, Prints and Photographs Division, Barbara Natanson, for her help regarding illustrations.

Particular thanks are due to John Marsden of the Manchester & Lancashire Family History Society for his help and assistance. I would also like to thank authors Angela Buckley, Mark Crail, Michelle Higgs and Jane Odiwe for their encouragement and advice; Else Churchill of the Society of Genealogists; and Gerard Lodge.

I would also like to express my gratitude to Rupert Harding of Pen & Sword Books for his help and encouragement.

Any errors or omissions are the author's own. Every effort has been made to trace copyright holders for images used in this work. The publishers welcome information on any attributions which have been omitted.

Last but not least, thank you to my husband Nigel, and my children Elizabeth and Gareth, for their help and support.

ABBREVIATIONS

Archives Hub	http://archiveshub.ac.uk
ARCHON	Archives Online Directory
AVRO	A.V. Roe and Co.
CCALS	Cheshire and Chester Archives and Local Studies
CL	Chetham's Library
FFHS	Federation of Family History Societies
FHS	Family History Society
GMC	Greater Manchester County
GMCRO	Greater Manchester County Record Office (with Manchester Archives)
GMLives	Greater Manchester Lives catalogue www.gmlives.org.uk/
GRO	General Register Office
IGI	International Genealogical Index
JRL	John Rylands Library, University of Manchester
LA	Lancashire Archives
LCAS	Lancashire and Cheshire Antiquarian Society
LCRS	Lancashire and Cheshire Record Society
MCC	Manchester City Council
MCL	Manchester Central Library
MCL(G)	GMCRO collections (GB.124) at MCL
MCL(M)	Manchester Archives and Local Studies collections (GB.127) at MCL
MG	*Manchester Genealogist*
MIs	Monumental Inscriptions
MLFHS	Manchester & Lancashire Family History Society
MLIA	Manchester Libraries, Information and Archives
MOSI	Museum of Science and Industry, Manchester
NWFA	Northwest Film Archive
RC	Roman Catholic
SCA	Salford City Archives
SLHL	Salford Local History Library

THSLC	Transactions of the Historic Society of Lancashire and Cheshire
TNA	The National Archives, Kew
TNA Discovery	TNA online catalogue http://discovery.nationalarchives.gov.uk/
UMIST	University of Manchester Institute of Science and Technology
UoM	University of Manchester
UoMARC	University of Manchester Archives and Records Centre
UoS	University of Salford Archives and Special Collections

INTRODUCTION

This book is a guide to family history and local history sources for the cities of Manchester and Salford. The author hopes that genealogists and local historians will find it useful for reference even if they are already experienced researchers.

The main chapters of *Tracing Your Manchester and Salford Ancestors* briefly discuss the origins and history of each city's religious and civic institutions, transport systems and major industries, along with relevant sources for extending your research. Suggestions for further reading are listed within the text and at the end of each chapter. Chapter 2 is an overview of basic family history sources for those readers completely new to genealogy; seasoned campaigners may still find it helpful as it includes the most up-to-date online resources.

The book concludes with several appendices: a directory of Manchester and Salford archives, libraries and academic repositories, and databases of family history and heritage societies, useful websites, and places to visit which bring the area's past to life. There's also a timeline of key dates. The MLIA website was under reconstruction at the time of going to press, so web pages may have changed since then. There is an online directory of collections here, www.manchester.gov.uk/directory/135/archive_and_local_collections, or if a URL fails visit the main MLIA page www.manchester.gov.uk/ info/448/archives_ and_local_history#/ and follow the links.

Manchester became a city in 1853; Salford achieved city status in 1926. For the purposes of this book, 'the city of Manchester' is defined as the area within the current city boundaries (post-1986, when the unitary authority of Manchester City Council was created). At present it stretches from Crumpsall, Blackley and Moston in the north, to Wythenshawe in the south. Its western boundary is contiguous with Bury, Salford and Trafford; to the east, Oldham, Tameside and Stockport.

The 'city of Salford' is also defined as the area within the current city boundaries and comprises Salford, Eccles, Worsley, Irlam and

Cadishead, and Swinton and Pendlebury. The River Irwell still marks the boundary with Manchester.

Readers are alerted to the most important resources in those instances where records are scattered across several archives. Boundary, administrative and diocesan changes are discussed where necessary.

The author was born in Salford, and is keenly aware that her native city is not a satellite of its neighbour on the opposite side of the River Irwell. Their histories are often interlinked, though, so to avoid needless repetition, the two cities are discussed together rather than in separate chapters.

Readers wishing for further information on family and local history sources for places in Greater Manchester outside the cities of Manchester and Salford – i.e. Bolton, Bury, Oldham, Rochdale, Stockport, Tameside and Wigan – should consult the author's *Tracing Your Lancashire Ancestors* (Pen & Sword, 2012). However, archives and resources within the Greater Manchester area are included in *Tracing Your Manchester and Salford Ancestors* if they contain important collections relating to either city.

Chapter 1

BEGIN EXPLORING THE PAST

TWO CITIES – SHARED HISTORIES

For centuries, the only link between Manchester and Salford was the 'Old Bridge' across the Irwell. This medieval structure witnessed heavy fighting during the Civil War when Manchester – which was staunchly Parliamentarian – was besieged by Royalist forces. Salford remained true to Charles I, its lord of the manor.

When Salford Old Bridge was rebuilt in 1838, it was renamed the Victoria Bridge in honour of the recently crowned queen. A visitor in the early 1840s who paused on the bridge for a moment would see the venerable tower of the Collegiate Church, and Chetham's College on one side of the Irwell. On the other bank, though, huge brick chimneys belched forth smoke.

The Industrial Revolution had accelerated the growth of both towns: coal mining, textiles, commerce, iron foundries, to name just a few of the many new opportunities that attracted thousands of migrants looking for work. As a result, the ink-black waters of the river stank from factory effluent, sewage and worse. However, the elegant villas of Salford Crescent enjoyed a beautiful landscape view, albeit somewhat marred by the huge bleach works by the river.

If the visitor crossed Victoria Bridge and continued into Manchester, he could explore the ancient streets round the old church, and admire the Ionic elegance of the Corn Exchange. And he could hardly fail to be struck by the huge number of palatial-sized warehouses in this booming commercial district.

When Queen Victoria visited the city in 1851, her arrival exemplified the progress made in the industrial age. She arrived at Patricroft station by train, then travelled along the Bridgewater Canal to Worsley Hall on a specially built royal barge. Next day, thousands of schoolchildren in Peel Park sang the national anthem to the royal visitors. All Manchester and Salford turned out to see their monarch as her carriage crossed Victoria Bridge and entered the city through a triumphal arch.

But behind the scenes, the poorer inhabitants of both towns suffered from dreadful living conditions in the 'back-to-back' terraced houses, and this poverty continued into the twentieth century. Diseases were rife and infant mortality high.

Manchester and Salford were also home to several famous scientists, writers, artists and politicians: John Dalton and James Prescott Joule, Thomas de Quincey, Joseph Brotherton, Richard Cobden, L.S. Lowry, Elizabeth Gaskell and Emmeline Pankhurst to name just a few.

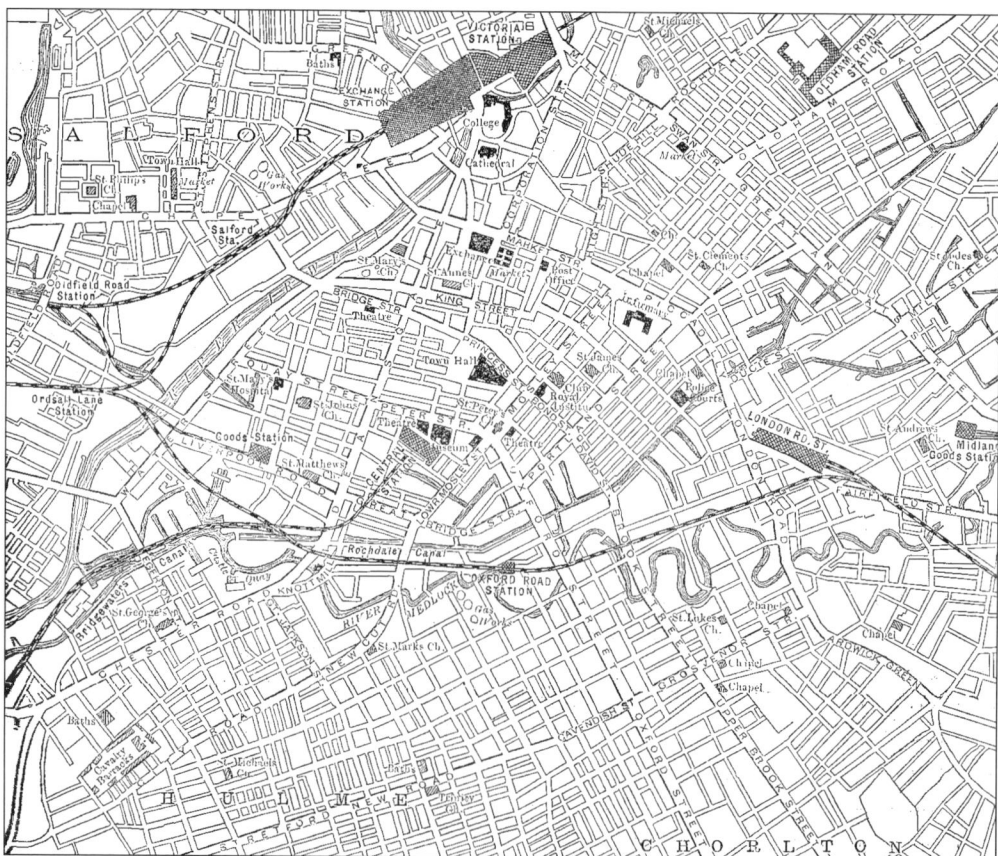

Map of central Manchester, 1880s. Our Own Country (*Cassell & Co., n.d., c.1883), Vol. III. (Author's collection)*

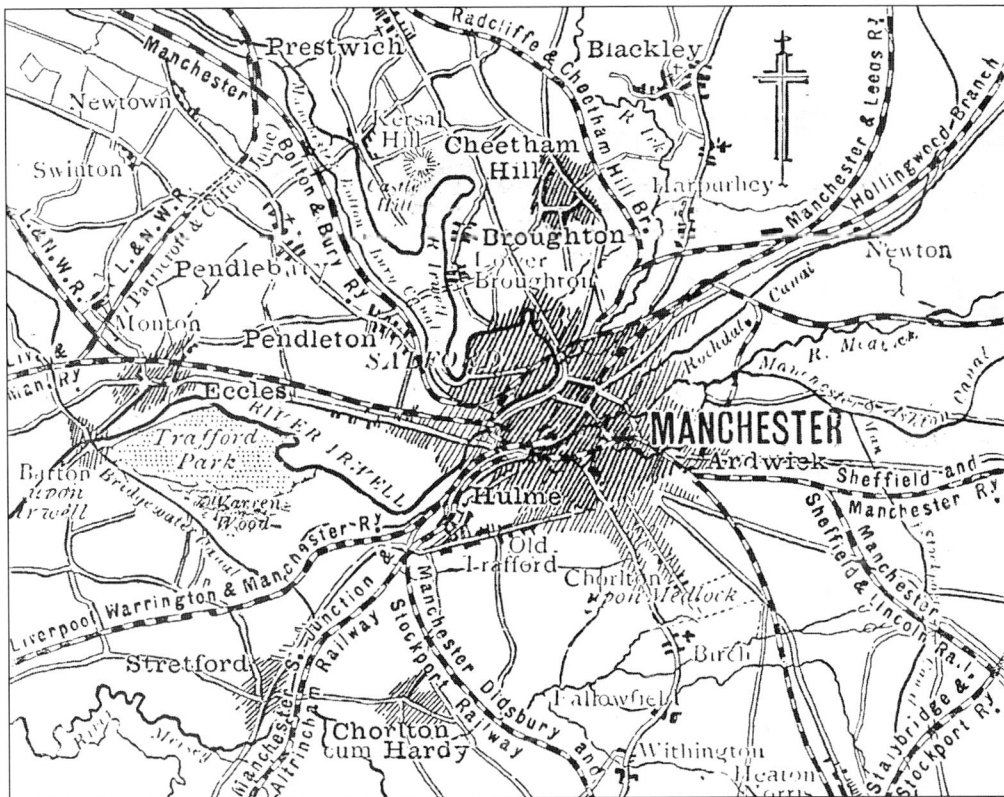

Map of Manchester and its environs, 1880s. Our Own Country *(Cassell & Co., n.d., c.1883), Vol. III. (Author's collection)*

In both world wars, thousands of men from Manchester and Salford answered the call to arms; women took over men's jobs to aid the war effort. The suffragettes' long quest for justice finally bore fruit after the war was over. During the Second World War, both cities endured the horrors of the Blitz.

Although the cities' industries have declined since their glory days, and many historic buildings have disappeared, reminders of the past can still be seen such as Heaton Hall, Ordsall Hall and Manchester Cathedral. Continuing migration into the area has led to a thriving multiculturalism, and many new buildings are appearing; the story of Manchester and Salford is by no means over.

HOW TO USE THIS BOOK
Use the Index and the sub-headings on the Contents pages to help navigate your way around the text. Abbreviations for the names of the

principal archives and libraries are listed in the next section and at the beginning of this book.

As so much information is now online, this book includes many websites. In order to save the reader from typing out long, complicated web addresses, in several instances the author has used the URL (website) shortener, bitly.com. Wherever you see a web address beginning with 'bit.ly' in this book, just type in the letters and numbers as given, and the website should appear (unless it has moved or expired since publication).

ARCHIVES, LIBRARIES AND REPOSITORIES

Several archives and record offices hold materials relevant to Manchester and Salford family history. Although the listings in this book are as up to date as possible, collections may have moved, or archives' contact details and websites may have changed since publication. Also, the archives or libraries mentioned may have reduced their opening hours or closed, owing to the current unprecedented public sector cutbacks.

Therefore, before travelling you should check the archive or library website or contact them to find out when it is open, and also if the collections you wish to consult are available. Special collections may be held off-site and may require ordering in advance, so allow at least two weeks' notice. If you cannot visit in person, most archives offer a research service (fee payable).

Although every effort has been made to highlight the most important resources for each topic in this work, readers are encouraged to explore the archives' and libraries' collections for themselves. However, bear in mind that records for the person, family, institution or business you seek may not have survived.

Most of the archives listed in this book have online catalogues, but cataloguing is an on-going process and some records may not yet be listed online. You may have to consult an archive's card and paper catalogues in person (or contact the archivist if distance makes this impossible) to find the records you seek.

The principal archives, libraries and resources for Manchester and Salford history and family history are listed below; more archives are mentioned where appropriate in the following chapters. Full contact details and key online links for these archives are listed in Appendix 1.

Cheshire and Chester Archives and Local Studies

The Cheshire and Chester Archive and Local Studies Service (CCALS) at Cheshire Record Office in Duke Street, Chester, cares for historical records and local studies collections for the ancient and modern county of Cheshire, and the diocese and the city of Chester.

The archive holds collections related to families, estates, railways, canals, Poor Law, electoral registers, census records, trade directories, maps, etc. Explore family history materials such as parish registers and local newspapers on microfilm. You can search Findmypast's Cheshire collection and Ancestry's Library Edition via its public computers. http://archives.cheshire.gov.uk.

Chetham's Library

Founded in 1653, Chetham's Library (CL) is the oldest public library in the English-speaking world. As well as over 100,000 printed works, the library holds medieval manuscripts, prints, broadsides, newspapers, trade directories and periodicals, especially relating to the Manchester area. Archives of businesses and notable local people and families include the Asshetons of Middleton and the Leech family of Manchester. Other important archives include the Belle Vue Zoological Gardens collection, and the Mullineux image collection amassed by local historians Frank and Elsie Mullineux of Walkden. The Champness Collection and Richard Hill Collection have archival, printed and photographic materials on transport and industrial history. Visitors should book an appointment; give at least one day's notice. www.chethams.org.uk.

John Rylands Library, University of Manchester

The University of Manchester Library on Deansgate is home to the former Victoria University of Manchester's special collections as well as the collections of the John Rylands Library (JRL). The library has a world-class collection of books including over 4,000 incunabula (early printed books). Its Special Collections include hundreds of records of companies, business associations, trade unions, charities, religious institutions, etc. Family papers include the Byrom family, Elizabeth Gaskell Manuscript Collection (MS), Jevons family and more. Estate records, charts, maps and deeds. The Library holds the *Manchester Guardian* (now the *Guardian*) and *Manchester Evening News* archive. www.library.manchester.ac.uk/rylands/.

Lancashire Archives

Lancashire Archives (LA) is the archive for the historic county of Lancashire. The Record Office's huge collections include parish registers, quarter sessions records, censuses, wills and probate, schools, Poor Law, family and estate records, manorial records, taxation, electoral registers, palatinate records, court records, etc. www.lancashire.gov.uk/libraries-and-archives/archives-and-record-office.aspx. There's also a local studies reference library.

See Reginald Sharpe France, *Guide to the Lancashire Record Office* (Lancashire County Library, 1985) and Janet D. Martin (ed.), *Guide to the Lancashire Record Office Supplement 1977–1989* (Lancashire County Library, 1992).

Manchester Cathedral Archives

The records of Manchester's ancient parish church. The parochial records (1573–twenty-first century) include parish registers from 1573 onwards, churchwardens' accounts and donations to the church: Mancath/1. See Chapter 2 for the best way to access the cathedral parish registers. The Capitular Records (1361–twenty-first century) are the records of the Warden and Fellows of the Collegiate Church of Manchester, and later, the records of the Dean and Chapter of Manchester Cathedral.

This collection includes minutes of Chapter meetings, financial records, title deeds, estate records, tithe leases, maps, plans, surveys and related papers of the Chapter Estates: Mancath/2. This series includes the Commonwealth Survey of 1649: Mancath/2/A/3/1. The personal papers of Bishops, Deans, Canons and members of staff from 1870 to *c*.2004 are in series ManCath/3. At least one week's notice is required to access items from the collections, which are produced for viewing at Chetham's Library (order in advance). www.manchestercathedral.org/history/archives.

Manchester Central Library

Manchester Central Library (MCL) is home to the city's lending and reference collections, and two major archives. Special collections and rare books can be viewed in the search room.

The MCL search room is the access point for Manchester Libraries, Information and Archives collections (ARCHON code GB.127), and throughout this book the abbreviation MCL(M) refers to these

Manchester Central Library. (© Sue Wilkes)

collections. (The GB.127 archive is referred to as Manchester Archives and Local Studies on TNA Discovery.)

Greater Manchester County Record Office (GMCRO) collections (ARCHON code GB.124), also available via the search room, will be referred to as MCL(G) throughout this work.

Use the Greater Manchester Lives catalogue (GMLives) to find the reference numbers for archival materials, www.gmlives.org.uk. Choose whether to search by 'images only' or 'archive collections'. Some materials are held off-site and at least two weeks' notice may be required to access them.

The two archives at MCL have major photographic collections. The Manchester Local Image Collection includes over 80,000 photos; you can buy A4-sized prints, http://bit.ly/1yEo5uP.

The Documentary Photographic Archive has 100,000 images of local businesses, family albums and school photos; purchase images from the collection online, http://bit.ly/2860EPr.

The Archives+ area on the ground floor of MCL is a one-stop shop for family history materials including parish registers on microfilm, censuses, trade directories, electoral registers, reference books, maps, newspapers, online access and exhibitions. The Local Studies reference library is on the same floor. The Manchester & Lancashire Family History Society has a help desk at MCL which is manned by volunteers daily. Local history books, collections on microfilm and local maps can be viewed without making an appointment, www.manchester.gov.uk/info/448/archives_and_local_history.

Manchester Libraries, Information and Archives

The Manchester Libraries, Information and Archives (MLIA) service includes over twenty Manchester City Council libraries, www.manchester.gov.uk/libraries. Family history materials are available via the libraries' public computers. It's a good idea to book a computer in advance; at Manchester libraries, usually the first hour is free, and you are limited to a 2-hour session.

Northwest Film Archive

The Northwest Film Archive (NWFA) is part of Library Special Collections at Manchester Metropolitan University, and is one of the partner organizations of Archives+ at MCL where it is now located. Holding over 40,000 items of film and video made in or about the region, the archive covers Greater Manchester, Merseyside, Lancashire, Cheshire and Cumbria, and includes cinema newsreels, documentaries, advertising and promotional material, educational and travel films, home movies and BBC regional programmes. Themes covered include work and industry, leisure, sport and entertainment, local traditions and community activities, transport, housing and wartime experiences. www.nwfa.mmu.ac.uk.

Salford City Archives

Home to the administrative records for Salford City, Salford City Archives (SCA) holds parish, Poor Law, township and school records. Important industrial collections include Nasmyth and Wilson & Co. Ltd. Family collections, e.g. the Leigh family of Worsley and the Egerton family (Earls of Ellesmere). SCA's collections are accessed at Salford Local History Library (below).

Salford Community Libraries

Limited history collections and reference works; the main local history collection is at SLHL (below). Salford Libraries' computers are free to use. www.salfordcommunityleisure.co.uk/libraries.

Salford Local History Library

Salford Local History Library (SLHL) is located within the Salford Museum and Art Gallery building on the ground floor and has an extensive local history reference collection. Family history material including census returns, maps (from 1848), newspapers (from 1858), street directories for Manchester and Salford; and a collection of 70,000 photographs. The library is currently digitizing its photographic collection and some images are now online, http://www.salford. photos/. www.salfordcommunityleisure.co.uk/culture/locations/salford-local-history-library.

University of Salford Archives and Special Collections

University of Salford Archives and Special Collections (UoS) include playwright Arthur Hopcraft's papers (AHP), Bartington Hall papers (BAR) and the Richard Badnall papers (RBP). The Walter Greenwood collection includes many photos of Manchester and Salford, 1860s–2004: WGC. www.salford.ac.uk/library/archives-and-special-collections.

Some collections, including the photographic collection, have been digitized and put online: Salford Archives Repository Collection. http://usir.salford.ac.uk/archives.

The National Archives, Kew

The National Archives (TNA), formerly the Public Record Office, hold millions of records relating to people, families, places, businesses, crime, censuses, transport, industry, etc. Collections of Lancashire records (including Manchester and Salford) at TNA are discussed in Walford D. Selby, *Lancashire and Cheshire Records Preserved in the Public Record Office*, Lancashire and Cheshire Record Society, Vols 7 and 8 (London, 1882, 1883).

Older reference works on genealogy may mention the National Register of Archives index, the Access to Archives (A2A) database and the ARCHON online directory of archives. These three online databases are now incorporated within TNA's Discovery Catalogue: http://discovery.nationalarchives.gov.uk.

If searching for a particular archive, go to http://discovery.national archives.gov.uk/find-an-archive and follow the online instructions. To find records for a particular person, go to the online catalogue, click on 'Find A Person', type in their name and limit your search by date, location or collection.

REFERENCE WORKS

The earliest known history of Manchester is Richard Hollingworth's *Mancuniensis*, written in the mid-1650s, during the English Civil War. Chetham's Library holds the original, and you can read it online: https:// chethams.org.uk/collections/digital-resources/hollingworths- mancuniensis/.

Since Hollingworth's day hundreds of histories of the Manchester area and the historic county of Lancashire have been published which can help put your ancestors' lives in context. Manchester City Council (MCC) libraries and Salford Community Libraries hold a good selection of this vast amount of literature. The following works are listed as a starting point; more are given at the end of this chapter.

The *Victoria County History of Lancaster* (VCH), in eight volumes (edited by W. Farrer and J. Brownbill, various dates), was published in the early twentieth century. The VCH contains detailed ecclesiastical, economic and civil histories of places in the historic county of Lancashire, www.victoriacountyhistory.ac.uk/counties/lancashire. Each chapter includes many references to original sources. Several volumes are available free at British History Online, www.british-history.ac.uk. Vol. 3 includes the early history of the Collegiate Church of Manchester (later the Cathedral). Vol. 4 has detailed local histories of Manchester, Salford and townships such as Blackley, Newton and Pendlebury.

John Heywood's *Manchester Historical Recorder* (1874) is a chronological list of significant events from AD 500, when the area was a 'wild and unfrequented woodland', to 1874. It includes the foundation dates and closures of many churches and chapels, technological changes, businesses, the names of important personages, political events and causes célèbres in Manchester and Salford. Unfortunately, the book has no index, but a searchable version (digital download) is available from Anguline Archives, http://anguline.co.uk.

John Aikin, *A description of the Country from thirty to forty miles round Manchester* (John Stockdale, 1795) is copiously illustrated and contains several maps. Aikin's book was reprinted by David & Charles in 1968.

See also W.A. Shaw's *Manchester Old and New*, 3 vols (1894), an illustrated history of the area's churches, industry and civic changes, which includes Salford.

For early twentieth-century local worthies, see W.T. Pike (ed.), *A Dictionary of Edwardian Biography: Manchester and Salford* (Edinburgh, 1987) (a facsimile reprint of part of Pike's 1899 work, *Manchester and Salford at the close of the 19th century*). Some pages from the book (with portraits and photos) are on the Archives+ Flickr page, bit.ly/20Zm MGT. Thomas Swindell's *Manchester Streets and Manchester Men*, 5 vols (J.E. Cornish, 1906–8) explores the city's history, including Salford.

The *Manchester Region History Review* includes book reviews and a bibliography of recently published works about the region's history. The magazine is published annually by the Manchester Centre for Regional History at Manchester Metropolitan University's Department of History, Politics and Philosophy. Free copies are available online, https://www2. mmu.ac.uk/hpp/mcrh/manchester-region-history-review/.

Salford has not been as well served by historians as Manchester, although it is mentioned in many of its neighbour's histories, as noted previously. See F.A. Bruton, *History of Manchester and Salford*, County History Reprints, (S.R. Publishers, 1970); T. Bergin, D.N. Pearce and S. Shaw, *Salford: A City and Its Past* (City of Salford, 1989); and Charles Hampson, *Salford Through The Ages* (E.J. Morten, 1972).

Salford LifeTimesLink, a twice-yearly magazine devoted to the city's heritage, history, museums, people and memories, is published by Salford Museum and Art Gallery. Past issues are available from the Salford Community Leisure website, http://bit.ly/1bIx7k1.

Many family pedigrees and historical records for northwest England have been published by groups such as the Chetham Society, Lancashire and Cheshire Record Society (LCRS), Historic Society of Lancashire and Cheshire, Lancashire and Cheshire Antiquarian Society (LCAS), Lancashire Parish Register Society and the Record Society. For example, court leet records, medieval records, Monumental Inscriptions (MIs), probate indexes and parish register transcriptions are just some of the types of record you can find in print. MCL and SLHL have copies of these publications.

For published resources on Manchester and Salford records, families and occupational sources, see Stuart A. Raymond, *Lancashire: A*

Genealogical Bibliography, 3 vols (Federation of Family History Societies, Birmingham, 1996). Although now somewhat out of date, it is still worth exploring to help you open up fresh avenues of research. Vol. 1 covers administrative records, estate and family papers, parish histories, directories, occupational sources, censuses and census substitutes, etc., listed alphabetically by area. Vol. 2 lists parish registers (including non-parochial), MIs, will transcripts and indexes. Vol. 3 covers heraldry, family histories and pedigrees. Each volume has an author index, place-name index and family name index.

• The Internet Archive, https://archive.org/index.php, and Google Books, https://books.google.co.uk/, often have free copies of old history books and historical record publications if they are out of copyright.
• The Connected Histories website covers online British History Sources, 1500–1900, and includes a family history guide. You can search its databases by keyword, name, place and date, www.connectedhistories.org/Default.aspx.
• The British Library has a large collection of books on Lancashire history. Its manuscripts collection includes many deeds and charters relating to Manchester, Salford and the historic county of Lancashire, www.bl.uk.
• The Manchester UK website has an online bibliography for books about the Manchester and Salford area (some out of print), www.manchester2002-uk.com/arts/books.html.

NEWSPAPERS IN LIBRARIES AND ONLINE
Local newspapers are a fantastic resource. As well as family notices such as births, weddings, deaths and funerals, they also reported detailed accounts of crimes, court proceedings, inquests and bankruptcies. You may find a school or sporting photo of your ancestor, or an exam result, or your ancestor may have been a member of a local club. The national press also reported major news stories from the provinces such as colliery disasters and scandals.

The earliest Manchester newspaper was seemingly the *Manchester Weekly Journal* (1719), printed and sold by Roger Adams. Henry Whitworth's *Manchester Gazette* appeared in 1730; seven years later, it changed its name to the *Manchester Magazine*. Another *Manchester*

Gazette was published by William Cowdroy from 1795; it underwent several changes of ownership before closing in 1829.

One of the longest-lived publications was Joseph Harrop's *Manchester Mercury*, first published on 3 March 1752. Harrop would meet the Derby mailcoach so he could get a 'scoop' on the latest news from London. After Harrop's death in 1804, his son Joseph continued the paper until John Edward Taylor bought it in 1825 and changed its name to the *Manchester Mercury and Tuesday's General Advertiser*. It ceased publication on 28 December 1830.

The earliest local newspapers contained little regional news; they mostly printed a digest of major news from the capital. However, they printed local advertisements: useful if you are researching local businesses as they included names and addresses.

As time went on, the amount of local news increased, and the editorials became more politicized. The *Manchester Herald*, a Radical newspaper, appeared in 1792 but ceased publication the following year after its premises were destroyed by a 'Church and King' mob. In 1821 cotton merchant John Edward Taylor launched the liberal *Manchester Guardian*, which flourished and later became a national newspaper – and institution.

MCL has a large selection of local newspapers on microfilm on the ground floor. The website has an A–Z listing of titles and dates available, http://bit.ly/2hV5A4S. A small number of titles are not available on microfilm and must be pre-ordered before visiting.

Salford did not have its own separate newspaper until 1859 (the *Salford News*, later the *Salford Weekly News*). The *Salford Chronicle* appeared a decade later. SLHL holds several historic Salford newspapers on microfilm (with some gaps), and has an extensive collection of newspaper cuttings. The library holds the *Eccles & Patricroft Journal*, 1874–1985; *Salford City Reporter* (*Salford Borough Reporter* up to 1926), 1880–2007; *Salford Weekly News*, 1859–84; and the *Swinton & Pendlebury Journal*, 1934–85.

A public library ticket (you can join online) gives you access to free 'online reference libraries', which you can explore via your home Internet connection. These electronic resources usually include encyclopedias, official government publications and historic newspapers.

MCC Libraries offer online access for members to the *Guardian*, previously the *Manchester Guardian*, 1821–2003 and *Observer*, 1791–

2003. A separate search engine gives full access to *The Times* Digital Archive, 1785–2003. The 'Newsbank' searchable database lets you explore a selection of international and regional titles, including the *Manchester Evening News*, from five to twenty-five years old, depending on the title, http://bit.ly/1TYegoE. The *Manchester Mercury* can be accessed free on the British Newspaper Archives website at any MCC Library by registering and logging in with your email address.

Salford Community Libraries offer access to free online resources such as the *Oxford Dictionary of National Biography*; newspapers are not currently included, http://bit.ly/1TRDbNI.

Lancashire Libraries offer online reference e-resources, www.lancashire.gov.uk/libraries-and-archives/libraries/digital-library.aspx. Members can also access *The Times* Digital Archive, 1785–1985, the British Library 19th Century Newspaper Collection and the Burney Collection of 17th–18th Century Newspapers online from home, www.lancashire.gov.uk/libraries-and-archives/libraries/digital-library.aspx#newspapers.

If local libraries do not hold the particular newspaper you seek, the largest collection of British newspapers is held by the British Library. The collection, formerly at Colindale, is now at Boston Spa, West Yorkshire. The collection is also available on microfilm in the Newsroom at the British Library's St Pancras site.

Many of the British Library's newspaper collections have now been digitized and can be searched online at British Newspaper Archives, www.britishnewspaperarchive.co.uk/. The website is free to search, but you must pay to view digitized images. Currently, the *Manchester Courier and Lancashire General Advertiser*, 1825–1916, *Manchester Evening News*, 1870–1945, *Manchester Mercury*, 1752–1830, and the *Manchester Times*, 1828–1900 are available. At the present time, no Salford newspapers are online, but new titles are being added all the time.

The *London Gazette* newspaper published legal notices such as bankruptcies, military promotions and gallantry awards. Its website is searchable by name, date, location or type of notice. If you find a published legal notice concerning one of your ancestors, you can download the page as a free PDF, or purchase a copy of the *Gazette*, https://www.thegazette.co.uk/.

FAMILY HISTORY, HERITAGE AND LOCAL SOCIETIES

It's a good idea to join a local history or family history society, especially if you are a new researcher. Societies often hold talks with guest speakers, and may have specialist libraries. Members are often extremely knowledgeable and keen to share their expertise, and it's an opportunity to make friends. Family history societies usually have online groups or forums with 'surname interests', so you can see if other people are researching the same families. Appendix 3 has contact details for local history and heritage groups, and family history societies.

Manchester & Lancashire Family History Society

Manchester & Lancashire Family History Society (MLFHS) is one of the UK's largest and longest established family history societies. Its website is an excellent starting point for your research, www.mlfhs.org.uk. Free research guides are available, www.mlfhs. org.uk/guides/index.php. The website also has several free searchable databases including Manchester 'strays', war memorial inscriptions, Manchester Crematorium obituaries, memorial inscriptions, Roman Catholic (RC) churches in Manchester and Salford, a RC register index, and much more. Complete data for some databases is restricted to members only: www.mlfhs.org.uk/data/onlinedata.php.

The society publishes *Manchester Genealogist* (*MG*); MCL and SLHL hold back copies. A limited number of articles from past issues are available online, www.mlfhs.org.uk/articles/article_index.php. MLFHS members can access back copies of the magazine from 2004 to the present day via the society's website. New members receive a family history fact-pack with tips on general genealogy research, and specialist resources for Manchester and Lancashire. The society and its branches hold regular meetings, with talks related to family history.

Society of Genealogists

The society (www.sog.org.uk), the largest in the UK, has a comprehensive library of genealogical materials such as published parish registers for Manchester Cathedral. It also has some unique collections of family history materials unavailable elsewhere. The society holds regular courses and talks. Non-members can access the library with a day pass or hourly pass. You can search the library catalogue online, www.sog.org.uk/the-library.

One-Name Studies

If you are researching a particular surname rather than compiling a family tree, consider joining the Guild of One-Name Studies. There's a surname search on its website, http://one-name.org/.

GENEALOGY SUPPLIERS

Researching your ancestors can be an expensive hobby. Luckily there are free resources available online, so if money is tight, explore those first before paying for expensive certificates. Some free websites are highlighted in the main text, and a further selection is listed in Appendix 4.

As mentioned earlier, library members can access some genealogy suppliers via library computers. Ancestry's Manchester Collection focuses on parish registers, but censuses and trade directories, military records, etc., are also available. Findmypast's Manchester Collection includes parish registers, cemeteries, industrial school registers, prison registers, rate books, school admissions and more.

Alternatively, if you wish to research in comfort at home, you can purchase a subscription service or 'pay to view' individual records. The main genealogy suppliers usually let you do a basic search for free, and then you choose whether to pay to see an image of the original document or not. If you register with a supplier (free), then you will receive updates about seasonal offers (e.g. a 'free trial), especially around Armistice Day in November.

The subscription websites constantly update their databases, so more record collections may have been added since publication. The subscription service you choose will depend on which databases are most relevant to your family tree.

You can also purchase books and CD-ROMs of census records, parish registers, maps, etc., from various online suppliers. The MLFHS online bookshop in particular has many publications relevant to Manchester and Salford, www.mlfhs-shop.co.uk/.

MAPS AND PLANS

Maps are essential for tracing lost buildings, institutions, farms, roads, etc., especially if used in conjunction with trade directories. A map will help put your ancestors' lives in context. For example, you can look for the nearest church, school or factory to your ancestors' home. If you find an ancestor in the censuses (Chapter 8), with relatives living in the nearby area, a map can show you how close they were to one another.

The earliest known map of Manchester and Salford is a plan dated 1650, http://bit.ly/1Sw58Uu. It shows the two towns surrounded by fields and gardens. A century later, John Berry's plan shows the green fields had been supplanted by many new streets and buildings on both sides of the River Irwell, http://bit.ly/1TOMA75. See J. Lee, *Maps and Plans of Manchester and Salford, 1650 to 1843: A handlist* (John Sherratt, 1957).

MCL has a large collection of maps, including the Ordnance Survey series from 1848 onwards, http://bit.ly/2i50ICY. The search room has a selection of maps on CD-ROM (no appointment needed), including historical maps from the early 1740s onwards, nineteenth-century Ordnance Survey town plans and Lancashire maps, and fire-insurance plans of the city centre. See 'Manchester in maps and the family historian', *MG*, Vol. 23 (3), 1987, pp. 167–72. Tithe maps, which are incredibly detailed, are discussed in Chapter 7.

The University of Manchester Library's online image collections include old maps of Manchester and Salford, http://bit.ly/1UZcHdc. British History Online has a series of Ordnance Survey 1:25,000 maps for Manchester and its environs, including Salford, for the late 1800s to early 1900s, www.british-history.ac.uk/os-1-to-2500/manchester.

The MLFHS website has a 'street search' for the Alan Godfrey series of reproduction Ordnance Survey maps of old Manchester and Salford (central Manchester *c.*1848, and Manchester and its environs 1889–1932). These extremely detailed maps (36in to 1 mile) show individual buildings such as churches and pubs. If you find the street you want, you can order the appropriate map from the MLFHS online shop: www.mlfhs.org.uk/data/godfrey_search_form.php.

For help with parish boundaries see J.P. Smith, *The Genealogists' Atlas of Lancashire* (Henry Young and Sons, Liverpool, 1930), available on CD-ROM from some genealogy suppliers.

The Gazetteer of British Place Names (Association of British Counties) has a searchable place-name index. The online listing for each location gives a grid reference and the administrative areas associated with each place. www.gazetteer.org.uk/.

The Vision of Britain website has historical statistics including photos, gazetteers, maps, related websites, etc. It has a useful overview of administrative districts and boundaries (click on 'Units and Statistics') with source references:

- Manchester: www.visionofbritain.org.uk/place/791.
- Salford: www.visionofbritain.org.uk/place/326.

If researching a particular location, check if it is included in the Register of One-Place Studies, http://oneplacestudy.org/england/index. html. The register looks at all historical aspects of each place. New places are being added all the time; you could register your own one-place study.

DISTANT MEMORIES

Published diaries, journals and memoirs are all excellent ways of exploring the past, although only a tiny sample can be listed here. See, for example, Craig Horner (ed.), *The Diary of Edmund Harrold, Wigmaker of Manchester 1712–15* (Ashgate Publishing, 2008). For an early eighteenth-century Manchester diarist, see Richard Parkinson (ed.), The *Private Journal and Literary Remains of John Byrom*, Chetham Society, Old Series, Vols 32 and 34 (1854–5).

Weaver Samuel Bamford, an author and veteran of Peterloo, also kept a journal; see M. Hewitt and R. Poole (eds), *The Diaries of Samuel Bamford* (Sutton Publishing, 2000). For early twentieth-century Salford, see Robert Roberts, *The Classic Slum* (Penguin Books, 1990) and *A Ragged Schooling* (Fontana Paperbacks, 1982), by the same author.

You can find more published diaries via the public library catalogues, and unpublished diaries and journals are listed in the archive catalogues of several repositories listed in this book. CL has a good collection of manuscript diaries.

Oral histories are another wonderful way to evoke the past. The Greater Manchester Sound Archive at MCL(G) has over 50,000 catalogued items, www.archivesplus.org/news/greater-manchester-sound-archive/. You can listen to over 1,200 recordings at MCL without making an appointment; a catalogue of this selection of the collection is online in spreadsheet format, http://bit.ly/1qNsnUf. Some recordings are available online, https://soundcloud.com/archivesplus.

This collection includes the BBC Radio Manchester Archive and the Salford Lifetimes Archive of over 200 recordings about the city and its people. The full catalogue will be on GMLives in late 2016 (search using 'Oral History'); currently the catalogue includes memories of Bradford Pit, wartime, immigration experiences, etc.

Old-Style Dating

If you are new to exploring historical records, and need to consult documents earlier than 1752 (such as parish registers), remember that 'Old Style' dating was then in use. The official new year began on 25 March (Lady Day) until 1 January 1752, when the 'New Style', our present mode of dating, was introduced. To convert an Old Style date to New Style, use this calendar converter, http://people.albion.edu/ imacinnes /calendar/Old_%26_New_Style_Dates.html.

There's more help on understanding old documents on TNA website, www.nationalarchives.gov.uk/palaeography/quick_reference.htm.

Pre-Decimal Currency, Imperial Weights and Measures

Before decimal currency was introduced in 1971, there were 12 pennies (*d*) to 1 shilling (*s*), and 20 shillings to 1 pound (£) (1 shilling equals 5p in post-decimal currency). A guinea was worth 21 shillings.

Distances were measured in feet, inches and yards: 12 inches (in) to 1 foot (ft), 3 feet to 1 yard (yd) (0.91m) and 1,760 yards to 1 mile. Weights were measured in pounds (lb) and ounces (oz): 16oz to 1lb, and 14lb to 1 stone. There were 112lb to 1 hundredweight (cwt), and 20cwt to 1 ton. For volumes, 1 pint (568ml) is still used for beer and cider; 2 pints make 1 quart, and 4 quarts equal 1 gallon.

Access to Records

Archives and repositories restrict access to records relating to persons who are (or may be) still alive if they contain personal information as specified by the Data Protection Act.

Sensitive records, for example, details of persons living in institutions, or who were in local authority care, or children who were adopted, are usually closed for up to 100 years. School archives that still hold their own records such as admission registers may only operate a thirty-year closure rule.

Each archive operates its own policy, and access may be at the archivist's discretion; proof may be requested that the relative concerned is deceased. If you are researching a close relative, access may be granted to a closed record if you make a written request under the Freedom of Information Act, https://www.gov.uk/make-a-freedom-of-information-request/the-freedom-of-information-act.

An archive's catalogue normally specifies the length of time for which records are closed to public access; contact the archivist if you are unsure whether access to a particular document is restricted.

FURTHER READING

Bates, Denise, *Historical Research Using British Newspapers*, Pen & Sword, 2016

Beesley, Ian and de Figueiredo, Peter, *Victorian Manchester and Salford*, Ryburn Publishing Ltd, 1988

Blanchard, Gill, *Tracing Your House History*, Pen & Sword, 2013

Blanchard, Gill, *Writing Your Family History*, Pen & Sword, 2014

The Changing Face of Manchester (no author), 2 vols, Manchester Evening News Syndication, 2006

Frangopulo, N.J. (ed.), *Rich Inheritance: A Guide To The History Of Manchester*, Manchester Education Committee, 1961

Kidd, Alan, *Manchester*, 3rd edn, Edinburgh University Press, 2002

Redding, Cyrus, Beard, J.R. and Taylor, W.C., *Pictorial History of the County of Lancaster*, George Routledge, 1844

Rogers, Colin Darlington and Smith, John Henry, *Local Family History 1538–1914*, Manchester University Press, 1991

Schofield, Jonathan, *Manchester Then and Now*, Batsford, 2009

Stephens, W.B., *Sources for English Local History*, Cambridge University Press, 1994

Tomlinson, V.I., *Salford In Pictures*, E.J. Morten, 1981

Worthington, Barry, *Discovering Manchester*, Sigma Leisure, 2002

Wyke, Terry, 'Nineteenth Century Manchester: A Preliminary Bibliography', in A.J. Kidd and J.W. Roberts (eds), *City, Class and Culture*, Manchester University Press, 1985

Wyke, Terry and Rudyard, Nigel, *Bibliography of North West England Vol. 14*, Directory of Local Studies in North West England, 1993

Chapter 2

FAMILY HISTORY BASICS

Before you begin your research, check which family documents you already own. Make copies of records held by other family members. Interview older relatives about places where your family may have lived, worked or gone to school. Were any of your relatives in the armed forces? Note down the names of any regiments or places where they served. Remember that information passed down through the generations may be inaccurate or confused.

CIVIL REGISTRATION

The most accurate way to compile a family tree is by working backwards in time through each generation, usually beginning with civil registration certificates. There's a guide on the Society of Genealogists' website, www.sog.org.uk/learn/help-getting-started-with-genealogy/ guide-three.

On and after 1 July 1837 in England and Wales, every birth, marriage and death had to be registered. Marriages could now be performed at register offices as well as churches. Each registration district had a Superintendent Registrar who kept records of all these events, and compiled an index to them in case of future queries. For a fee, you can order copy certificates of the entries made by the registrar (see below for Manchester and Salford registration services).

A birth certificate for events prior to 1969 shows the location and place where a person was born, name, sex, father's name (if known), mother's maiden name and address, father's occupation, date when the birth was registered, and name and address of the person who registered the birth. After 1969 both parents' place of birth was included on a person's birth certificate and, after 1984, the mother's occupation was added.

A marriage certificate gives the date of the wedding, the place where solemnized, bride's name and groom's name and occupation, residences at time of marriage and name and occupation of bride's and groom's fathers. The bride and groom sometimes gave their planned future address to avoid paying for two sets of banns. If the bride had been married before, the marriage certificate should show all her previous surnames. Similarly, the groom's details should mention if he was a widower.

It was not uncommon for people to marry two or even three times during their lifetime as mortality rates were formerly much higher than today. See Rebecca Probert, *Marriage Law For Genealogists* (Takeaway Publishing, 2012) and *Divorced, Bigamist, Bereaved?* (Takeaway Publishing, 2015), by the same author.

A death certificate (pre-1969) states the person's age and occupation, date of death and address, cause of death, date when registered and the informant's name and residence. After 1837 no person could be buried without a death certificate except stillborn children (after 1875 certificates were required for these babies, too). After 1969, the deceased person's place and date of birth was included on the certificate.

Two sets of indexes are available for birth, marriage and death certificates (BMDs): local and national, and you need to know the index reference number so that you can order the correct certificate.

Local Indexes

The indexes compiled by local registrars are the most accurate. An index of civil registration districts, with dates of boundary changes, is available on the UKBMD website: www.ukbmd.org.uk/genuki/reg.

The boundaries of a particular registration district were not necessarily the same as the town or city it was based on. The original districts were based on the Poor Law unions (see Chapter 5), so they often cover a much larger area than the town they were first named after.

Manchester Registration District went through several boundary changes between 1837 and 1974, www.ukbmd.org.uk/genuki/reg/districts/manchester.html. Then on 1 April 1974, it became part of the Greater Manchester County Registration District following the creation of the new county. John A. Coupe, *A Guide To The Registration Districts of Manchester* (MLFHS, 2010) lists the boundary changes from 1837 to the present day for Manchester, Chorlton-upon-Medlock and Prestwich (with maps).

MANCHESTER REGISTRATION SERVICE: COPY CERTIFICATES

The service is responsible for the records of births, deaths, marriages and civil partnerships registered in the city of Manchester from July 1837 to the present day. However, MCL holds all birth, marriage and death registers, 1837–1915 for the city (not Salford), and issues copy certificates for this date range, http://bit.ly/1XF65SF.

Virtually all pre-1915 indexes are now on the Lancashire BMD website, www.lancashirebmd.org.uk. A successful search of the index elicits a reference number, which you use to order a copy certificate from MCL. You can collect the certificate in person, or ask for it to be posted to you (usually five working days). You can also order in person at MCL, or by post. No priority service is available for pre-1915 certificates.

A BMD certificate for an event post-1915 must be ordered from Manchester Register Office, http://bit.ly/1SfiMhu. You can apply online, by post or in person. For a birth certificate, you will need the child's name, date of birth, place of birth (address or hospital) and one or both parent's names. For a marriage certificate, you will need the name of both people, date of marriage and location (i.e. church or venue). Both partners' addresses are needed for a civil partnership certificate. For a death certificate, the office requires the deceased's name, date and location of death. Alternatively, you can make an appointment to make a general search of the local indexes yourself at the Register Office (fee payable) – contact the office for further details.

Table 1: Civil Registration: Areas Included in the City of Manchester

Ancoats	Clayton	Moss Side	Woodhouse Park
Ardwick	Collyhurst	Moston	Wythenshawe
Baguley	Crumpsall	Newall Green	
Benchill	Didsbury	Newton Heath	
Beswick	Fallowfield	Northenden	
Blackley	Gorton	Northern Moor	
Bradford	Harpurhey	Openshaw	
Burnage	Hulme	Peel Hall	
Charlestown	Levenshulme	Rusholme	
Cheetham	Longsight	Sharston	
Chorlton	Miles Platting	Whalley Range	
City Centre	Moss Nook	Withington	

Manchester Register Office can only supply certificates for those persons born within the city boundaries existing at that date. This means that you can't order a certificate for someone born in a district of Manchester that was not part of the city then, even if it is now. You must check which registration district they were living in at the time.

SALFORD REGISTER OFFICE

BMD certificates for Salford (including Eccles, Pendlebury, Swinton and Worsley) from 1837 onwards can be ordered from Salford Register Office either online, by telephone, in person or by post, www.salford. gov.uk/births-marriages-and-deaths/family-history/copy-certificates/. There's a list of places within Salford Registration District and boundary changes on the UKBMD website, www.ukbmd.org.uk/genuki/reg/ districts/salford.html.

GRO Indexes

Another set of indexes to BMDs was compiled by the General Register Office (GRO). Each quarter, local registrars sent copies of their records of births, marriages and deaths to the GRO, which created its own indexes. Because the GRO indexes are not the same as the local indexes, you cannot use a local register office index reference number to order a certificate from the GRO, or vice versa. Also, since these records were copies of the local register entries, they are not as accurate as the local ones because mistakes were sometimes made. However, they can be the easiest way of finding an ancestor's record if you have no clues to the location.

The GRO indexes, formerly called the St Catherine's House indexes, are divided into quarters for each year and give the location where the birth, marriage or death was registered. The indexes are on the GRO website, https://www.gro.gov.uk/gro/content/certificates/default.asp. The earliest quarter available is for July–September 1837. Use the volume and page number references in the index to order a copy certificate from the GRO (see Appendix 2) at Southport via its website or by post, https://www.gov.uk/order-copy-birth-death-marriage-certificate.

The information included in the GRO indexes became more detailed over the years. For example, after 1866 a person's age at death was included in the indexes. This means that if wished you can calculate an approximate date of birth and order a birth certificate without first paying for a death certificate. A mother's maiden name was not included in the birth indexes until 1911. Surnames of husband and wife (maiden name) were not listed within the same marriages index until 1912. The GRO also looks after the Adopted Children Register (for adoptions on or after 1 January 1927). See Karen Bali, *Researching Adoption: An essential guide to tracing birth ancestors and relatives* (Family History Partnership, 2015).

Local record offices and reference libraries may have microfilm copies of the GRO indexes; the government website has a list of holders, https://www.gov.uk/government/publications/public-holders-of-the-general-register-office-indexes.

MCL has copies of the GRO indexes for births, 1837–2013; marriages, 1837–2013; deaths, 1837–2013; overseas, 1761–2013; civil partnerships, 2005–13; and adoptions, 1927–2013. Some indexes are on microfiche, i.e. births and deaths for England and Wales, 2006 to September Quarter 2015; and marriages, 2006–13. MCL does not hold any divorce records.

The GRO indexes can be searched on the FreeBMD website (the whole index has not yet been transcribed), www.freebmd.org.uk. The major genealogy suppliers offer access to the GRO indexes; as noted earlier, the Ancestry and Findmypast sites are free via MCC library computers. Findmypast also has the index to Divorce and Matrimonial Causes, 1858–1903.

Unfortunately, you may have trouble locating a civil registration record for your ancestor. Sometimes mistakes were made in the indexes, or your relative might have been recorded in a neighbouring district. Some people did not bother to register their children's births – there were no penalties for non-registration until 1874. If you cannot find a GRO index reference for your ancestor, the GRO is normally willing to conduct a search within a limited timeframe for the event. See Colin Darlington Rogers, *The Family Tree Detective* (4th edn, Manchester University Press, 2008) for step-by-step solutions to solving difficulties in your family tree.

The next stage should be to see if a record of the event was made in a parish register. From 1538 onwards, parish registers were the official records for baptisms, marriages and burials, and they are one of the best ways to research your family tree.

ANGLICAN PARISH REGISTERS

In Tudor times, Thomas Cromwell instituted proper record-keeping for baptisms, weddings and burials in each parish. After September 1538, the clergy recorded each event in a parish register, which was stored securely in a chest. Unfortunately many of these early records were lost as they were only written on paper. At the end of the sixteenth century, the registers were recorded on parchment instead. However, parish registers often have 'gaps' during the Civil War years (1641–52) as they were not maintained regularly during that era of huge social upheaval.

Parishes also sent copies of their registers to the bishop of the diocese. These 'bishop's transcripts' were made annually and are very useful if the original register is missing. Sometimes names or dates were copied incorrectly; however, the transcript may have family information not noted in the register, and vice versa. The original bishop's transcripts are usually, but not always, kept at the diocesan record office.

Hardwicke's Marriage Act of 1754 required parishes to keep records of banns and marriages in special books of printed forms; each page had four forms. All weddings – except those of Quakers and Jews – were solemnized in an Anglican church.

More regulation followed in 1812. George Rose's Act required the date, occupations and residence of the parents to be noted in addition to their names when a child was baptized. When a person was buried, the date, deceased's age and place where they lived was now included. Churchwardens' accounts may include payments made for burials, too.

Marriage registers, depending on the date, show the names of the couple, their signature (or 'mark' if illiterate), their age, marital status, place of residence and the names of two witnesses (often related to the happy couple). After 1837 the names of the father of the bride, and groom, were included.

Original parish registers are deposited with the diocesan record office (usually the county record office), unless they are still in use at their original church.

Marriage Bonds, Allegations, Licences

Normally, couples were married after the banns had been read on three successive Sundays before their wedding day. However, sometimes a couple got married by special licence, e.g. if the bride or groom was a minor, or they wanted to marry away from home.

If a licence was applied for, the couple needed to fill in some forms: marriage 'bonds' and 'allegations'. In the 'allegation', the couple (or bride or groom) alleged that there was no reason, such as a previous marriage, or a too-close blood relationship, why they could not marry legally. A 'bond' set a high financial penalty which the groom (or a close relative) agreed to pay if the allegation was later discovered to be untrue.

For example, on 5 September 1609, Adam Holme and Jane Tompson of the parish of Manchester applied for a marriage licence, and their 'bondsman' was Richard Thorp of Salford (spellings and punctuation as per the original): 'The man had his mothers consent & the maide had neither father nor mother, & att her own disposeing, and that hee did not talk wth the mans father, butt verily beleeved there was no Impedmt.' (W.F. Irvine (ed.), *Marriage Licences Granted Within the Archdeaconry of Chester*, 2 vols (LCRS, 1907), Vol. I, *1606–16*).

CCALS holds marriage bonds and allegations for the diocese of Chester (which included Manchester and Salford) from the seventeenth century onwards (ED) and (EDC 8): indexes are available. LCRS has published indexes to the bonds and allegations held by CCALS, and MCL has copies.

THE PARISH OF MANCHESTER

Prior to 1540, the ancient parish of Manchester was in the diocese of Lichfield, but was controlled by the archdeacon of Chester. After the Reformation, the parish lay in the vast diocese of Chester, which was split into twelve deaneries, one of which was Manchester. The parish, which comprised several townships, was in Salford Hundred (see Chapter 7). The British History Online website has an index map of Manchester parish, www.british-history.ac.uk/vch/lancs/vol4/pp174-187.

CCALS holds the records for the Archdeaconry of Chester (but not the original wills for Lancashire residents), including consistory court books, 1502–1976 (ED), marriage, wills and tithe cases (EDC 1), ecclesiastical court papers, 1525–1860 (EDC 5) and marriage act books, 1606–1945 (EDC 7).

Manchester Collegiate Church (Cathedral)

The earliest written record of Manchester's churches appears to be William the Conqueror's Domesday Book of 1086. Two churches are

Manchester Collegiate Church interior. Gallery of Engravings, *Vol. II (Fisher, Son & Co., c.1845). (Author's collection)*

mentioned, St Mary's and St Michael's, and they held a 'carucate' of land (about 120 acres). Their precise location is uncertain, but it appears likely that St Mary's was on or near the site of the modern Cathedral. St Michael's is thought by historians to have been located at Ashton-under-Lyne.

In medieval times, the lords of the manor (see Chapter 7) appointed the rector of Manchester. The La Warre family became barons of Manchester in the early fifteenth century, and Thomas La Warre was made rector. Because the previous rectors did not live in the town, the parish was in a parlous state and the old church was neglected. In 1421 Thomas La Warre, who was now lord of the manor, too, founded a 'college' of a warden and eight fellows to care for the parish. Sir John Huntingdon was the first warden.

The 'Collegiate Church' was endowed with lands, and a brand new building was erected. Local worthies and merchants beautified the new church; for example, the Stanley family built the chapter house.

The college was dissolved during Edward VI's reforms, and the Stanley family took over its lands and patronage. Mary I re-established the college, but it was in an impoverished state until Elizabeth I granted it a fresh charter. The college comprised one warden, four priests, two vicars and four lay persons. It was renamed Christ's College (it was formerly dedicated to the Blessed Virgin) and its lands were restored. Charles I granted it yet another new charter in 1635; Robert Heyrick was the new warden. Aside from the Collegiate Church, there were several chapels-of-ease in Manchester, which later became parishes in their own right.

See John Prudhoe, *Heart of a City: A History of Manchester Cathedral* (Manchester Cathedral, 1966); Thomas Perkins, *The Cathedral Church of Manchester* (George Bell, 1901); and S. Hibbert-Ware, W.R. Whatton and J. Palmer, *The Episcopal See of Manchester: the foundations of Manchester: comprising the college and collegiate church, the free Grammar school and Chetham's hospital* (T. Agnew, 1848).

Now if your ancestor lived in the parish of Manchester prior to the mid-nineteenth century, it's highly likely that they were baptized or married at the Collegiate Church. This is because its warden and fellows believed that its charter entitled them to claim a fee when a person was baptized or married at any church within the parish. This meant that people had to pay two fees, one to the incumbent of their church of

Manchester Cathedral from the southeast. Our Own Country *(Cassell & Co., n.d., c.1883), Vol. III. (Author's collection)*

choice – and the Collegiate Church. So it was obviously cheaper to have the ceremony at the Collegiate Church, because then they only paid one fee – an important consideration for the town's many impoverished working families. In the 1830s the additional fees received by the Cathedral were 6*d.* for a baptism; 1*s.* 4*d.* to bury a child under the age of 7 years; 1*s.* 10*d.* to bury a person over the age of 7 years; 3*s.* for each marriage by banns; and 7*s.* for each marriage by licence.

There was a shortage of churches in Manchester, too. This led to the custom of 'batches' of ceremonies taking place on the same day. Strangers to the town often popped in to the Collegiate Church to see the amazing (and often extremely noisy) spectacle of these mass weddings and christenings. See H.S. Cunningham, 'Married at the Collegiate and Parish Church of Manchester', *MG*, Vol. 34, Issue 4 (MLFHS, 1999) (available online, http://bit.ly/26qZMnG); 'Marriage in the Cathedral' (no author), *MG*, Vol. 39, Issue 1 (MLFHS, 2003) (http://bit.ly/1rwL9PW); and G. Wilkie, 'Manchester Collegiate Church Again', *MG*, Vol. 52, Issue 1 (MLFHS, 2016).

In 1847 the diocese of Manchester was created. The Collegiate Church became a cathedral, dedicated to St Mary, St Denys and St George, and the seat of a bishop in the province of York. The Right Revd James Prince Lee was enthroned as bishop at the Cathedral on 11 February 1848. The new diocese comprised the archdeaconries of Manchester and Lancaster; the archdeaconry of Manchester was composed of the deaneries of Manchester, Blackburn and Leyland. So to sum up, the city of Manchester was now the seat of the diocese within the deanery and archdeaconry of Manchester. When the diocese of Blackburn was created in 1927, the diocese of Manchester was reduced even further.

In 1850 the Parish of Manchester Division Act reduced the size of the parish and it was split into smaller parishes the following year. However, changes to the Cathedral's income could not be made until there was a new incumbent, so in practice, double fees for its parishioners who wanted to marry elsewhere in the parish continued until the mid-1870s.

By 1860 the former ancient parish had been split into over sixty parishes. Then in 1866 the townships of Manchester parish became parishes in their own right. Manchester parish's modern extent is just 1 square mile in the city centre.

• Familysearch has a list of Manchester Cathedral pre-1851 chapelries, https://familysearch.org/wiki/en/A_Comprehensive_List_ of_All_Pre-1851_Manchester_Parishes_and_Chapelries.
• Gerard Lodge has a useful overview of Manchester city centre churches on his website, www.manchester-family-history-research.co.uk/new_page_11.htm.

Other Churches in Manchester and Salford
The oldest church within the present-day City of Salford is probably St Mary's, in the ancient parish of Eccles, which dates back to at least the fourteenth century. However, the town of Salford had no church of its own for many centuries (although the Radclyffe family had a private chapel at Ordsall Hall).

Thomas de la Booth founded a chapel on the Old Bridge across the Irwell during Edward VI's reign; it was rebuilt in 1505. After it became derelict it was used as a dungeon for malefactors; if the river flooded,

Church of the Sacred Trinity, Salford. The church was built c.1751 on the site of Salford Chapel, founded in 1634 by Humphrey Booth. Illustration by H.E. Tidmarsh, Manchester Old and New *(Cassell & Co., c.1894), Vol. II. (Author's collection)*

the poor prisoners risked being drowned. The dungeon was demolished in 1776.

In *c*.1634 Humphrey Booth built the Salford chapel, later Church of the Sacred Trinity, at his own cost and endowed it with lands. By the early 1750s the chapel had become unsafe and it was rebuilt in stone with a Gothic steeple.

There do not appear to have been any new churches in Manchester until St Ann's Church was founded by Lady Ann Bland of Hulme Hall. St Ann's was consecrated in 1712. St Mary's, built in the Doric style between Deansgate and the River Irwell, was consecrated in 1756. It was followed by St Paul's (1765), St John's on Byrom Street (1768), St Peter's (1788), St Michael's (1789), St James' (1788) and others.

Sacred Trinity stood alone in Salford until St Stephen's was built by the Revd Mosley Cheek and consecrated on 23 July 1794. Salford's next major Anglican church was St Philip's, 'a plain Grecian structure', on

Broken Bank in 1825. The first stone of Christ Church, on Acton Square, near Salford Crescent, was laid in 1830: it opened the following year. Its first rector was the Revd Hugh Stowell. Next to appear were St Matthias' Church on Broughton Road and St Bartholomew's on Oldfield Road, both in 1842, and more followed in the late nineteenth and early twentieth centuries as the town's population grew.

Several churches in Manchester and Salford which were originally in the parish of Manchester became district parishes during the nineteenth century. Also, some chapelries like Newton had their own ancient churches. For a more detailed history of these parishes, see Vol. 4 of the *Victoria County History of Lancaster*. Unfortunately, many fine old churches in the Manchester area were later demolished as their congregations dwindled. See J.S. Crowther, *An Architectural History of the Cathedral Church, Manchester* (J.E. Cornish, 1893); J.J. Parkinson-Bailey, *Manchester: An Architectural History* (Manchester University Press, 2000); and C. Hartwell, M. Hyde and N. Pevsner, *Lancashire: Manchester and the South East*, Pevsner Architectural Guides: Buildings of England (Yale University Press, 2004).

Parish Registers
The earliest surviving records for the Collegiate Church begin in 1573. The first baptism record is dated 3 August, for 'Elline daughter of Willm Darbie' (spellings as per the original). The earliest marriage to survive is for Nicholas Cleator and Elline Pendleton on 19 August, and the first burial is for Robert Fyssher, dated 1 August the same year.

The Cathedral's parochial registers include parish registers, banns books, churchwardens' accounts and sextons' registers, 1732–1848; the sextons' registers from 1753 onwards often give age of deceased and cause of death. The original registers are held by Manchester Cathedral Archives. However, the easiest way to access them is on Ancestry.co.uk, and on microfilm at MCL. MLFHS has created an index to the Cathedral's burial registers, 1573–1868 (available on Findmypast and on CD-ROM from the MLFHS online bookshop).

The original parish registers for other Manchester and Salford churches are held by MCL(M), but they are not usually produced for researchers unless microfilm or microfiche copies are unavailable. MLFHS has published a guide, *Registers In Manchester Archives and Local*

Studies (2011) (the 'Pink Book', currently out of print but available at MCL).

• Search a directory of parish registers available at Central Library, including Nonconformist and RC registers, and some Jewish records, www.manchester.gov.uk/directory/100/church_registers.
• A–Z directory of parish registers at MCL: www.manchester.gov.uk/directory/100/a_to_z.
• Guide to parish register collections at MCL: http://bit.ly/2h5EHwN.

Lancashire Archives also holds copies of some Manchester and Salford parish registers, including bishops' transcripts and MIs, on microfilm (and some transcripts).

• Manchester churches: www.lancashire.gov.uk/media/898370/M.pdf.
• Salford churches: www.lancashire.gov.uk/media/898378/S.pdf.

SLHL has some copies of parish registers for churches and Nonconformist chapels on microfilm or as hard copy.

The Lancashire Parish Register Society has published transcripts of parish registers in print and on CD-ROM, including the Cathedral (see Table 2 below), www.lprs.org.uk/.

Table 2: Lancashire Parish Register Publications

Church	Registers	Dates	Order Ref.
Manchester Cathedral (St Mary, St Denys and St George)	Baptisms, marriages, burials	1573–1616	CD 31
	Baptisms, marriages, burials	1616–53	CD 55–6
	Births	1654–62	CD 89
	Baptisms	1662–6	CD 89
	Marriages, burials	1653–66	CD 89
	Baptisms, marriages, burials	1666–1700	Vol. 183
St James', George Street, Manchester	Baptisms, burials	1788–1837	Vol. 134

St Mary's, Manchester	Baptisms	1756–1888	CD 77
	Marriages	1806–37	CD 77
	Burials	1754–1871	CD 77
Sacred Trinity, Salford	Baptisms, burials	1616–1837	Vol. 174
	Marriages	1635–1754	Vol. 174

FAMILYSEARCH (LATTER-DAY SAINTS) AND THE INTERNATIONAL GENEALOGICAL INDEX

The IGI is an index to parish registers (baptism, marriage and burial records including bishop's transcripts) and some census returns compiled by the Church of Latter-Day Saints. The index includes Lancashire marriages in the diocese of Chester, and summaries of census returns. MCL and SLHL have copies of the IGI, and you can also search it free on the Family Search website: https://familysearch.org/.

An interactive map (1851) allows you to explore ecclesiastical jurisdictions by parish, diocese, deanery, Poor Law union, civil registration district and more: http://maps.familysearch.org.

LANCASHIRE ONLINE PARISH CLERKS

The Lancashire Online Parish Clerks website is one of the best free family history resources, www.lan-opc.org.uk/. The website, which is updated regularly, has transcripts from over 8,000 parish registers including Manchester and Salford, as well as census records, cemetery records, MIs, etc., with photos and local histories. The website also has some transcriptions of RC registers. Browse the site by parish or location, or conduct an overall surname search; limit your results by life event (baptism, marriage, burial) or by father's, mother's or spouse's surname. Surname indexes are available for some parish registers.

• Some free transcripts of the Cathedral registers, 1573–1836 are available, www.lan-opc.org.uk/Manchester/Manchester/cathedral/index.html.
• Manchester Home Page: www.lan opc.org.uk/Manchester/index.html.
• Salford Home Page: www.lan-opc.org.uk/Salford/index.html.

JOHN OWEN MANUSCRIPTS

The John Owen manuscripts at MCL(M) form one of the most important sources for Manchester genealogists: MISC/687. These manuscripts (over eighty volumes) contain Owen's notes of parish register transcripts, family pedigrees, MIs, drawings of local landmarks, photos and information about local families.

The Owen manuscripts are on microfilm and indexes are available: MF566–581b. Findmypast has transcripts of the manuscripts for Gorton, Newton and Flixton from 1571–1785. See Ernest Axon, *Index To The Owen MSS* (Manchester, 1900). Axon's index is not fully comprehensive; MLFHS has published a booklet containing an updated index to the manuscripts. Over 200 images of Owen's illustrations, photographed by Gerard Lodge, are online on the Archives+ Flickr page, http://bit.ly/1IERKtf.

Burial, Cemetery, Cremation Records and Memorial Inscriptions
During the mid-nineteenth century, many city graveyards were permanently closed and new municipal ones were created further out of town. For example, Walker's Croft near St Michael's Church, which was used by the Collegiate Church for the burial of poor people for many years, was sold to railway companies for development in the 1850s. Very few original gravestones have survived in Manchester.

However, local historians and antiquarians recorded inscriptions from family gravestones before they were lost (see the John Owen manuscripts listing above), and some have been published by MLFHS. See J. Marsden, *Something You Should Know About Death and Burial* (MLFHS, 2004; a new edition is planned). MCL(M)'s collection of town clerks' records, 1690–1968 includes papers relating to closed burial grounds, including transcriptions: M74.

Bradshaw's *Illustrated Guide to Manchester* (Manchester, 1857), lists four cemeteries: Ardwick Cemetery on Ford Street (1838); Rusholme Road (1821), used by Dissenters; Harpurhey on Rochdale Road (also known as Manchester General, opened in 1837); and New Barnes Cemetery (Weaste) on Eccles New Road, Salford (1857). Philips Park Cemetery opened in 1866; Southern Cemetery in 1879; Gorton Cemetery in 1900; and Blackley Cemetery in 1953.

Cremation became a popular alternative to burials after the mid-1880s. Manchester had one of the first municipal crematoria, at Barlow

Moor Road in 1892. Unfortunately, its records perished in the Manchester Blitz of 1940. Cemetery and crematorium records are usually kept at the cemetery or crematorium office; a fee may be charged for conducting a search.

MCL has some MIs, and burial registers for Gorton Cemetery, Philips Park Cemetery, Manchester General Cemetery and Southern Cemetery on microfilm. There's an online guide to cemetery records and MIs, http://bit.ly/2hPsBq9.

The MLFHS website has a free guide to researching burials in the Manchester area, http://mlfhs.org.uk/guides/researching_burials_ mis. pdf. There's also a comprehensive (free) list of Manchester graveyards, www.mlfhs.org.uk/Infobase/graveyards.php. Another MLFHS database has details of burial grounds in the Greater Manchester area (including Salford) with notes on the location of surviving records or transcripts, www.mlfhs.org.uk/data/BurialGrounds-Mar18-1.pdf.

MLFHS members can access an index to transcripts of over 7,000 newspaper death notices and obituaries for persons cremated at Manchester Crematorium, 1892–1940 via the society's website (a limited free surname search is available); the collection is also on Findmypast. This collection also includes 109 cremations for 1894–1932 taken from the funeral records of R. Pepperdine, Funeral Directors, deposited at MCL(M).

The MLFHS website also has an index to over 189,000 names from over 48,000 memorials, as well an index to nearly ½ million burials in Manchester, Salford and Bolton cemeteries. (The full transcripts are only available to members but there is a limited free name search.) More MIs are currently being added, including details from the John Owen manuscripts, and the number of names in the index is expected to be greatly expanded in the near future.

For the history of Manchester graveyards, see John Marsden, *Forgotten Fields: Looking For Manchester's Old Burial Grounds* (Bright Pen, 2014). Findmypast's Manchester Collection has burial records and MIs for Ardwick Cemetery, 1838–1950; Cheetham Hill Wesleyan Cemetery burial registers, 1815–1968; Rusholme Road burial registers, 1821–1933 and MIs; and Withington Workhouse death registers, 1857–1949 and interment registers, 1898–1922.

The Federation of Family History Societies (FFHS) has compiled a National Burials Index for England and Wales. The index gives the person, age, date, location and source so that you can look up the original document or transcription, www.ffhs.org.uk/burials/nbi-overview.php. Part of the index is available on Findmypast. Coverage currently includes some Manchester Cathedral burial records; St Ann's; St James' (George Street); and St Mary's on Deansgate.

MANCHESTER BURIAL RECORDS

This is a free searchable database for Blackley Cemetery, Blackley Crematorium, Gorton, Philips Park, Manchester General and Southern Cemeteries. You can search by name, location and date; you can also see if more than one person is buried in a particular plot. (Please note that the burial registers for Manchester General Cemetery before 1886 no longer exist, so these names have been lost.) A small fee is payable to unlock further information about a person's burial register entry: www.burialrecords.manchester.gov.uk/.

MANCHESTER GENERAL CEMETERY TRANSCRIPTIONS PROJECT

The project, run by volunteers, is transcribing the MIs at the cemetery, http://mgctp.moonfruit.com. The website includes photos of some headstones and notable burials with inscriptions, including some policemen and firemen. The transcriptions will be deposited at MCL when completed. There's a database of grave searches: http://mgctp.moonfruit.com/#/grave-searches/4569680988.

SALFORD BURIAL RECORDS

For grave searches in Salford, see the City Council website for cemetery contact details, www.salford.gov.uk/births-marriages-and-deaths/dealing-with-a-death/grave-searches/.

NONCONFORMISTS, ROMAN CATHOLICS AND OTHER FAITHS

Following the Act of Settlement, many Manchester and Salford families continued to practise Roman Catholicism (the 'old religion'). Although there were penalties for 'recusancy', Roman Catholics wished to be baptized and married according to the rites of their church. So your Catholic ancestors may have been baptized, or married, once in an Anglican church and again in a Catholic church in secret. (For recusancy fines, see series E 372, E 376, E 377 at TNA.)

In the early 1800s, there were just two RC chapels in Manchester – wholly inadequate for the area's growing population of Catholic families, many of them Irish migrants. The oldest, St Chad's, was founded in 1774 on Rook Street. The building was sold in 1846, and a new edifice built at Cheetham Hill; it was consecrated in August 1847. The other chapel, St Mary's, was built by subscription on Mulberry Street (1794). Salford had no RC place of worship until shortly before the foundation of the Catholic diocese of Salford in 1850; Dr William Turner was the first bishop. Salford's new Cathedral on Chapel Street was dedicated to St John the Evangelist; it opened in August 1848.

See R. Croskell, *Memoirs of Catholic Manchester* (North West Catholic History Society, 1997) and John O'Dea, *The Story of the Old Faith in Manchester* (London, 1910). For later Roman Catholicism in the area, see Steven Fielding, 'The Irish Catholics of Manchester and Salford: aspects of their religious and political history, 1890–1939', online PhD thesis (University of Warwick, 1988), http://bit.ly/1r53JO2.

The MLFHS website has a free list of RC churches in Manchester and Salford, with addresses and dates of their opening and closure, and name changes, www.mlfhs.org.uk/data/catholic_churches_in_manchester.php.

Roman Catholic Records

LA is the official place of deposit for RC registers for Manchester and Salford, although some registers may still be held at their original church.

For example, LA holds the records for St Chad's from its foundation until 1922, including school records (RCMC). It also holds St Mary's registers, 1794–1980, including baptisms, marriages and confirmations, school log books and the register of marriages, 1917–65 (RCMM).

• Manchester RC church registers, Guide 'M':
www.lancashire.gov.uk/media/67383/M.pdf.
• Salford RC church registers, Guide 'S':
www.lancashire.gov.uk/media/67398/S.pdf.

MCL has a limited collection of RC parish registers on microfilm. MLFHS is currently transcribing an index to Manchester and Salford Catholic registers; a searchable database is online, www.mlfhs.org.uk/data/catholic_search.php. This index contains over ½ million names of children, parents and godparents. The full data is only available on CD-ROM, available from the MLFHS online shop. The churches covered by the index, with sources and location of the original records, are also listed online, www.mlfhs.org.uk/data/catholic_churches.php/.

The Catholic Family History Society (www.catholicfhs.co.uk) has published Manchester parish registers on CD-ROM, currently for St Anne's (Junction Street); St Mary's (Mulberry Street), and St Patrick's (Livesey Street). The society has also published a database of Lancashire Catholic wills, 1492–1894, www.catholicfhs.co.uk/publications.html# datadisks.

The Salford Diocesan Archive at Manchester holds papers, manuscripts, correspondence, minute books, property deed index, printed material, books, photographic collection and memorabilia (not parish registers) for the diocese. It also holds records for the Carmelite Convent, the Catholic Teachers' Federation and some educational records (but very few admission registers), www.salforddiocese.net/ #!archives/cya8. The archive's holdings are summarized on TNA Discovery. Contact details are given in Appendix 2.

The former Talbot Library at Preston, which included collections on RC history, John Henry Newman and Irish studies, is now deposited with Liverpool Hope University's Special Collections, located in the Sheppard-Worlock Library. The department also holds the Gradwell Collection of RC studies and early printed works, www.hope.ac.uk/ gateway/library/specialcollections/collections/.

Methodists, Dissenters and Quakers
In the early 1700s, the only Dissenting chapel in Manchester was the Presbyterian chapel in Acres Field (later Cross Street), founded in 1693. The first minister was Henry Newcombe. A Jacobite mob wrecked the chapel in 1714; it was rebuilt in the late 1730s, and taken over by the Unitarians in 1775.

Methodism gained a particular stronghold in the area, probably owing to John Wesley, who preached in chapels on both sides of the River Irwell. William Brocklehurst built a fine chapel on Oldham Street (1780), and there were several more in the town. The Methodists also had a chapel at Gravel Lane in Salford, and another in Irwell Street (1826). In 1871 the old chapel on Oldham Street was replaced by Central Hall. This later became the headquarters of the Manchester and

Salford Wesleyan Methodist Mission, which took an active interest in looking after the district's poorer inhabitants. The Primitive Methodists also had chapels in Manchester and Salford.

Mosley Street was home to another Unitarian chapel (1789), and a handsome chapel belonging to the Independents (1788). In 1800 Revd William Cowherd founded the Bible Christians sect in a new chapel, Christ Church on King Street in Salford, which opened on 20 September. Cowherd's flock abstained from meat and intoxicating liquor: the foundation of the vegetarian and temperance movements.

The Society of Friends had a meeting house in Jackson's Row, Manchester, founded in 1732. By the early 1800s, however, it had been pulled down, although its burial ground was still in use. A new meeting house was built in Dickinson Street (1795), which also had a burial ground attached to it; in 1828 it was replaced by a new building in Mount Street.

TNA holds Nonconformist registers including those of Methodists, Wesleyans, Independents, Protestant Dissenters, Congregationalists and Quakers, www.nationalarchives.gov.uk/help-with-your-research/research-guides/nonconformist-non-parish-births-marriages-deaths-1567-1969/. TNA's official partner website for Nonconformist records for England and Wales, including some RC records, is BMD Registers, www.bmdregisters.co.uk.

Although Baptists, Salvationists and Quakers kept records of births, marriages and burials, they did not baptize their children. Because Nonconformists did not always have their own burial grounds, you may find they were buried in Anglican graveyards (sometimes a special area was reserved for them). The Society of Genealogists has a guide to Nonconformist records, www.sog.org.uk/learn/help-getting-started-with-genealogy/guide-seven.

Some original Nonconformist registers are still held locally, for example, LA has Salford Congregational Church records, 1855–1988 (CUSA), and it also has microfilm copies of Nonconformist registers. For full alphabetical listings of chapels and churches at LA see Guide M for Manchester, www.lancashire.gov.uk/media/898319/M.pdf, and Guide S for Salford, www.lancashire.gov.uk/media/898328/S.pdf.

MCL(M) holds records for Methodist, Baptist, Congregational (now United Reformed), Presbyterian and Unitarian places of worship for the city of Manchester and Salford, http://bit.ly/2gXo03p. There's an online guide to the archive's holdings of Methodist circuit records, http://bit.ly/2hViPCz. MCL(M) holds records of the Manchester and Stockport District, and its forerunners, the Manchester First District and Manchester Second District including minute books (M202). Many of these records are available via Ancestry.

Quaker records at MCL(M) include the Hardshaw East Monthly Meeting and the former Hardshaw Monthly Meeting (M85); both meetings covered the Manchester area. The records, from 1654–1952, include minutes, sufferings and distraints (fines), and membership records. Societies in this series include the Manchester District Preparative Meeting (M85/6) and the Eccles Preparative Meeting (M85/8). Quaker registers – births, marriages, burials, graves and deaths – for Hardshaw East and Hardshaw West (which included Liverpool and Chester) are available at MCL on microfilm.

The JRL is home to the Methodist Archives and Research Centre, the largest collection of Methodist Connexional records in the UK, which includes personal papers and other records of ministers, www.library.manchester.ac.uk/search-resources/guide-to-special-collections/methodist. You can browse images from JRL's Nonconformist collections online, http://bit.ly/21HqbKO.

In 1898 a fund-raising project – the 'Twentieth Century Fund' – was set up to commemorate John Wesley's death and to build Central Hall, Westminster. The names of persons who donated a guinea or more are recorded on the Wesleyan Methodist Historic Roll. MLFHS members can access a searchable database of almost 18,000 names from volumes 27–8 of the roll via the society's website.

See Richard Ratcliffe, *Methodist Records for Family Historians* (FFHS, 2014) and Philip Thornborow, *A Methodist in the Family?* (Methodist Publishing, 2014).

WILLS AND PROBATE BEFORE 1858

For centuries, a deceased person's will was proved in the appropriate ecclesiastical court. TNA has a guide, www.national archives.gov.uk/help-with-your-research/research-guides/wills-or-administrations-before-1858/.

Before 1541 Manchester and Salford were in the diocese of Lichfield, so any surviving wills will be at Lichfield Record Office. After 1541 Manchester and Salford were in the Archdeaconry of Chester, so wills were usually proved in that archdeacon's court (but see below for complex estates). The LCRS has published indexes and lists of wills and administrations proved in the consistory court of Chester and the archdeaconry of Richmond (which covered Lancashire north of the Ribble). There's a guide on the MLIA website, http://bit.ly/2gXIEkW.

Lancashire wills proved at Chester from 1487–1858 are held at LA (WC); few survive prior to 1541. In Chester diocese, wills for estates less than £40 in value were known as 'infra' wills, and those for estates of more than £40 in value were called 'supra' wills. 'Supra' wills were proved in the bishop's court (consistory court). Some early wills proved at Chester were damaged beyond repair; this is known because many missing wills were recorded in the bishop's registers or 'Act Books'. Abstracts of these wills were published by the Chetham Society.

The CCALS website has an online index of Cheshire residents' wills proved at Chester, 1492–1940, which you can use to order a copy of the will, http://archivedatabases.cheshire.gov.uk/RecordOfficeWillEPayments /search.aspx.

Complex Estates

If a person held property or land in more than one archdeaconry but within the same diocese, then probate was proved in the bishop's court. If an estate was scattered over more than one diocese, or the deceased left goods worth more than £5, then probate was granted by a senior court: the archbishop's prerogative court. For Lancashire, this was the Prerogative Court of York (PCY), because the historic county was in the ecclesiastical province of York. The Borthwick Institute, York holds the original PCY records which are indexed on Findmypast. Copies of wills can be ordered from Findmypast and the Borthwick Institute (see listing below).

The Prerogative Court of Canterbury (PCC), the most senior church court, was used if a person held property in the ecclesiastical provinces of York and Canterbury. The PCC records for 1384–1858 are at TNA (PROB 11), and they include the wills of many Manchester and Salford people. You can order copies online from TNA, www.nationalarchives. gov.uk/help-with-your-research/research-guides/wills-1384-1858/.

The Society of Genealogists has microfilm copies of will indexes and some abstracts of wills, and has published books of will indexes. The dates in the will indexes are the date when probate was granted; it sometimes took years to prove a will.

Death duty registers (IR 26 at TNA) are useful if you cannot find a will between 1796 and 1858. These registers (usually for estates worth more than £20) often contain detailed family information, www.national archives.gov.uk/help-with-your-research/research-guides/death-duties-1796-1903/.

Borthwick Institute for Archives

Borthwick holds probate records and wills for the Prerogative Court of York, Dean and Chapter of York, and Exchequer Court of York from 1359–1858; there is also a library. Copies of probate records can be ordered. The institute can search for up to five individuals free of charge so long as the name of testator/testatrix, abode and date of death/probate/burial is supplied. The volume/folio number of the probate record is helpful but not always required. If the above information is not supplied, a research service is available at a cost of £15 per half hour. There is a copying charge of £5 per entry for a registered paper or digital copy. Advanced booking to visit the archive is recommended, www.york.ac.uk/borthwick/.

WILLS AND PROBATE AFTER 1858

From 11 January 1858, responsibility for probate was taken away from ecclesiastical courts in England and Wales. Wills were proved in district probate registries instead; Manchester now had its own probate registry. MCL has the National Probate Calendar (index) on microfiche for 1858–1943 and from 1930–59 as hard copy. Ancestry has the National Probate index for 1858–1966. If you find a will for your ancestor in the index (calendar), it will tell you which probate court the will was proved in. Use this information to order a copy from Leeds District Probate Registry or the appropriate local district probate registry (see Appendix 2).

If you cannot find a will for your ancestor, possibly one was never made. If a person died intestate within the county palatine of Lancashire, and there were no obvious beneficiaries, then their estate was (and still is) given to the Duchy of Lancaster, rather than the Crown as is normally the case, as 'bona vacantia' ('vacant goods'), www.duchyoflancaster.co.uk/about-the-duchy/duties-of-the-duchy/bona-vacantia/. The proceeds go to charity.

DIVORCE RECORDS

Prior to 1858, a couple could not get a full divorce without a private Act of Parliament. TNA at Kew holds divorce records from 1858 onwards (J 77); there's an online guide, www.nationalarchives.gov.uk/help-with-your-research/research-guides/divorces/. Ancestry's collections include UK Civil Divorce records, 1858–1911. Family or solicitors' papers held in local archives may include correspondence or papers relating to divorce or separation.

FURTHER READING

Annal, David, *Easy Family History*, 2nd edn, Bloomsbury, 2013

Christian, Peter, *The Genealogists' Internet*, A. & C. Black, 2012

Fowler, Simon, *Family History: Digging Deeper*, History Press, 2012

Foy, Karen, *Family History For Beginners*, History Press, 2011

Gandy, Michael, *Catholic Missions and Register 1700–1880, Vol. 5 North West England*, Michael Gandy, 1998

Gibson, Jeremy and Churchill, Else, *Probate Jurisdictions: where to look for wills*, FFHS, 2002

Mitchinson, A.J., *The Catholic Family Historian's Handbook*, North West Catholic History Society, 1999

Osborn, Helen, *Genealogy: Essential Research Methods*, Robert Hale Ltd, 2012

Raymond, Stuart, *Birth and Baptism Records for Family Historians*, Family History Partnership, 2010

Raymond, Stuart, *Tracing Your Ancestors' Parish Records*, Pen & Sword, 2015

Scott, Jonathan, *The Family History Web Directory: The Genealogical Websites You Can't Do Without*, Pen & Sword, 2015

Shrimpton, Jayne, *Tracing Your Ancestors Through Family Photographs*, Pen & Sword, 2014

Symes, Ruth Alexandra, *Family First: Tracing Relationships in the Past*, Pen & Sword, 2015

Tate, W.E., *The Parish Chest*, 3rd edn, Cambridge University Press, 1979

Taylor, Nigel and Grannum, Karen, *Wills and Probate Records: A Guide for Family Historians*, TNA, 2009

Wilkes, Sue, *Tracing Your Lancashire Ancestors*, Pen & Sword, 2012

Chapter 3

THE TRANSPORT REVOLUTION

Manchester was renowned for its textile manufactures as early as the mid-sixteenth century, as we shall see later. However, Manchester's future role as 'Cottonopolis' was rooted in the great improvements to its transport links which grew up during the Industrial Revolution. Turnpike roads, canals and railways all played their part in making Manchester and Salford prosperous.

Before the mid-eighteenth century, merchants who wished to move their goods faced considerable obstacles. The region's roads were extremely poor, as many travellers testified in their diaries and letters. Covered waggons and saddle-horses struggled over 'roads' pitted with huge ruts which rain turned into dangerous traps for the unwary traveller. Most goods were moved using packhorses; obviously this greatly limited the quantity that could be moved in one go.

The Highways Act of 1555 put the responsibility for maintaining roads on each parish. Local magistrates appointed a surveyor of the highways (a post with responsibility but not remuneration). The parish's inhabitants were expected to help mend the roads ('statute labour') and could be fined for not doing so. If they completed the work as requested, then the justices of the peace certified this and rescinded the fine.

Even in central Manchester, the roads were so bad that no business person or well-to-do family kept their own carriage until Madame Drake of Long Millgate set up her carriage in 1758. Over time, local magistrates realized that one way to raise funds for road-mending was to fine the whole parish, not just individuals. In 1817, the parish of Manchester was fined the immense sum of £1,600 in order to repair Oxford Road. Records relating to road maintenance may be found in parish vestry records. Quarter sessions and assize records may include magistrates' orders for inhabitants to fulfil statute labour on the highway and indictments (or appeals against) non-payments of tolls.

TURNPIKE TRUSTS AND HIGHWAYS

Turnpikes became a popular method of upgrading roads locally. An Act of Parliament was required to set up a turnpike trust over a named section of road. The trust agreed to build and maintain the road, and was empowered to charge tolls to travellers who used it. A toll-bar was set up at each end of the road so that tolls could be collected. See S.W. Partington, *The toll bars of Manchester: including the toll bridges and the origin of our public institutions* (Neil Richardson, 1983).

The road to Stockport was probably the first in the Manchester area to be turnpiked, by the Manchester and Buxton Turnpike Trust (1725). Within three decades, several more roads were under the control of turnpike trusts.

The introduction of turnpikes, and better methods of road construction by innovators such as John Metcalf and, later, John Loudon MacAdam and Thomas Telford, improved travel times. In 1754, however, a 'flying coach' still took four-and-a-half days to reach London from Manchester. The town did not have a stagecoach service until 1760, when John Hanforth and his partners Matthew Howe, Samuel Glanville and William Richardson set up regular services to London and Liverpool. Merchants and traders could now reach the capital in three days, 'if God permit'. An inside seat for the journey cost 2*s*. 6*d*., and an outside seat was half-price. See Dorian Gerhold, 'John Handforth and Manchester's first stagecoaches', *THSLC*, Vol. 156, 2008.

By the late 1770s Pickford's flying coach took two days to reach London. And during Britain's lengthy war with France, when news broke of the Peace of Amiens in 1802, the *Defiance* and *Telegraph* coaches brought the longed-for tidings from the capital to Manchester within 24 hours (usually the run took 30 hours).

The General Turnpike Act of 1822 required trusts to register annual accounts with local justices at quarter sessions. Lancashire quarter sessions records at LA (QDT) include accounts for ninety turnpike trusts including Manchester and Salford routes (QDT/1).

MCL(M) has several series relating to turnpikes. Members of the Carill-Worsley family of Platt were trustees of the Rusholme Turnpike Trust, and the family's estate records include financial records (bills and accounts), 1793–8 for the trust (M35). The Highway Surveyor's records for Rusholme township, 1768–1808 include payments from inhabitants for statute labour for the road, and (after 1773) payments to the surveyor

Pickford & Co.'s Royal Fly-Van, c.1820. After a contemporary painting. Stagecoach and Mail in Days of Yore *(Chapman & Hall, 1903), Vol. II.*

of the Manchester to Wilmslow turnpike (M10/23). The records of the Manchester and Wilmslow Turnpike Trust, 1753–1883 include accounts, toll mortgages, trustees' minutes, parliamentary petitions, etc. (M124).

Turnpike records may be held at several locations. For example, the Hulme and Eccles Turnpike Trust was established in 1806 to create a road from Great Bridgewater Street, Manchester, across the Irwell and through Salford and Eccles. MCL(M) holds its records from 1807–66 including cash book, toll leases and mortgages, etc. (M54). Salford City Archives holds lists of debts incurred by the same trust, 1807–49 (L/CS/CL).

Tameside Local Studies and Archives hold correspondence, minutes and accounts for the Manchester and Ashton-under-Lyne Turnpike Trust (Acc2903), and the Manchester and Saltersbrook Turnpike Trust, 1732–1971 (TTM). Oldham Local Studies and Archives hold assorted financial records for the Manchester, Oldham and Co. Turnpike Trust, 1806–80 (M/18).

Turnpike roads were often used as convenient boundaries, so survey and estate records may also include references to them. Solicitors' papers sometimes include deeds and conveyances, leases, assignments of tolls, or plans of properties and land associated with turnpikes. For example, the Kenyon of Peel Collection at LA includes a late eighteenth-century map of the turnpike roads from Manchester to Liverpool, Wigan, Bolton, Preston and Lancaster after the Pendleton Turnpike Act (DDKE/Box52/29).

Whenever a private company or trust wanted to create a new thoroughfare such as a turnpike road, canal or railway, or plan building works or street improvements, then a map or plan was deposited with the local authority or clerk of the peace (quarter sessions records). For example, MCL(M)'s collection of deposited plans and sections created by Manchester Corporation (the 'Muniment Room Crates') covers 1875–1974 (M626).

CANALS

During the middle of the eighteenth century, the speedy movement of large cargoes such as coal was still difficult. Roads were virtually impassable in the winter months, which made food prices high, too.

An obvious solution was to send bulky cargoes by water. Following petitions to Parliament by Manchester merchants and drapers, an Act to 'canalize' the Rivers Mersey and Irwell was passed by Parliament in 1721. When it opened to shipping in 1736, the Mersey & Irwell Navigation made the Irwell navigable from Bank Quay at Warrington to Quay Street in Manchester for vessels of up to 50 tons. The Salford quay for the navigation was not completed until 1755, however. The Mersey & Irwell Navigation Company, which collected tolls from the vessels using the waterway, later became known as the Old Quay Company.

The Duke of Bridgewater and His Canal

Sending cargo by water was much cheaper than by road. It cost 40s. per ton to send goods by road, but only 10s. per ton by river between Warrington and Manchester. However, local mine owners like Francis Egerton, 3rd Duke of Bridgewater felt that his transport costs were far too high. The price of coal at the pit-mouth of his Worsley mine was 10d. per horse-load. By the time coal was carried to the River Irwell by pony or cart, loaded onto the boats, and unloaded again in Manchester, the price per horse-load had more than doubled. Even if the Duke used his own boats to transport his coal, the Mersey & Irwell Navigation Company charged him 3s. 4d. per ton, no matter how short the distance travelled.

The Duke decided to build his own canal between his collieries at Worsley Mill and Manchester. At first, the Duke and his land agent John Gilbert proposed to cut a short canal from Worsley mines to Hollin Ferry on the Mersey & Irwell Navigation, but instantly encountered opposition from that waterway's owners. However, the shortest route to Manchester involved crossing the valley of the River Irwell. Pioneering millwright James Brindley (1716–72) was asked to realize the Duke's vision. The new canal began deep inside the Worsley mines (it acted as a drain for the collieries), then soared across the valley along the mighty Barton aqueduct, 30ft in the air.

When the Bridgewater Canal opened on 17 July 1761, this spectacular engineering feat caused a sensation. The Duke and his gentlemen friends went to see water let into the cut, and a 'great number of spectators' assembled. 'As soon as the water had risen . . . a large boat, carrying 50 tons, was towed along the new part of the canal, over the arches, which were so firm, secure and compact, that not a single drop of water could be perceived to pass or ooze through' (*Annual Register . . . of the Year 1761* (London, 1762)). After the canal's completion the price of the Duke's coal fell from 7d. per hundredweight to 3d. per hundredweight, which was a great boon to the people of Manchester. By 1772 the Duke's boats were able to reach Liverpool.

The Duke of Bridgewater's Canal Company also ran packet services from the late 1760s, and the old Packet House can still be seen at Worsley. In 1807 the Old Quay Company tried to compete by running its own passenger service between Manchester and Runcorn.

Canal Mania

The success of the Duke's canal spurred on the building of more waterways: 'canal mania'. During the 1790s, the Manchester, Bolton & Bury Canal was built to carry coal from Kearsley and Clifton via Salford to Bolton and Bury's textile mills. The Ashton Canal, constructed during the same decade, linked Manchester and Ashton-under-Lyne. The first canal across the Pennines, the Rochdale Canal, was completed in the

Worsley Hall, on the Bridgewater Canal. Lancashire and Cheshire Past and Present *(William Mackenzie, London, n.d., c.1867), Div. I, Vol. 1. (Author's collection)*

early 1800s. The Manchester & Salford Junction Canal (1839) was only just over half a mile long. It connected the River Irwell (near the Old Quay) with the Rochdale Canal near the Albion Mills.

Several different types of vessel plied the northwest waterways, depending on their route and cargo. On the Bridgewater Canal, iron-hulled 'starvationers', 47ft long by 4ft 6in wide, transported coal to Manchester from Worsley; they carried up to 8 tons, and were crewed by men. 'Box boats' were used on the same canal; coal was loaded into containers holding 8cwt, with twelve boxes to each boat. The Bridgewater Canal Trust owned many barges and lighters called 'dukers' in honour of the Canal Duke.

'Flats' were huge flat-bottomed boats which carried cargo on rivers and on the canals. The Rochdale Canal was broad enough to take 'wide-beam' boats, and narrowboats also found their way onto Manchester's canals.

The advent of the railways (see below) inevitably led to a loss of canal traffic; some were taken over by railway companies. However, the age of canal building was not finished yet in Manchester.

The Manchester Ship Canal

During the 1880s Britain endured a long trade depression, and Manchester businessmen became frustrated by the port of Liverpool's virtual monopoly on cotton imports. They decided that a ship canal right into the heart of Manchester's industrial district was the best way to revitalize trade and industry.

The Manchester Ship Canal Company was formed in 1885; Daniel Adamson was the chairman. Two years later, the company bought the Bridgewater Canal and Mersey & Irwell Navigation; the former would link other waterways with the Ship Canal, and the latter would form part of it.

Thousands of navvies, men and boys, were employed building the 'Big Ditch'; 'steam' navvies helped move millions of tons of earth. Salford Docks (nos 6–9) accommodated large ocean-going ships of up to 15,000 tons; the 'Pomona' docks in Manchester (nos 1–4) were for coastal vessels and steamers.

This massive engineering challenge was beset by money and labour problems and accidents. After several years of construction, the Manchester Ship Canal Company faced financial disaster, but a last-ditch rescue loan of millions of pounds from Manchester Corporation in 1891 saved the day. Salford Corporation offered financial help, too.

When the 35-mile-long canal opened on 1 January 1894, the sun shone and thousands of people lined the banks of the canal; even the navvies wore their Sunday best. The canal was not an immediate success, but as time passed it brought much wealth, commerce and employment to Manchester and Salford. The Co-operative Wholesale Society was just one of the major firms that used the Ship Canal. Salford's population swelled as people flocked to work in the new factories. (See Chapter 4 for the development of Trafford Park.)

In the late 1930s, Manchester was still the fifth busiest port in the UK. But the advent of container vessels meant that the Ship Canal was no longer wide enough for modern vessels and traffic decreased from the 1970s onwards. Manchester and Salford Docks closed in the early

The Barton Swing Aqueduct, built c.1893. It carries the Bridgewater Canal over the Manchester Ship Canal. (© Sue Wilkes)

1980s and these once-bustling industrial heartlands became a symbol of urban decay.

The Canal Archive: 'Bridging The Years' website explores the building of the Bridgewater Canal and the Manchester Ship Canal, and the Trafford Park and Salford Quays area, www.canalarchive.org.uk/index.php. It has an online map of the canals in Manchester, Salford and Trafford, www.canalarchive.org.uk/map/staticIndex.php.

Many works have been published on canal history, and only a brief bibliography can be given here. For a detailed account of the growth of the canal network locally, see Charles Hadfield and Gordon Biddle, *The Canals of North-west England*, 2 vols (David & Charles, 1970); David E. Owen, *Canals To Manchester* (Manchester University Press, 1977); and Peter Maw, *Transport and the industrial city: Manchester and the canal age 1750–1850* (Manchester University Press, 2013).

For the Bridgewater Canal, see Glen Atkinson, *The Canal Duke's Collieries: Worsley 1760–1900* (Neil Richardson, 1998) and Samuel Smiles, *Brindley and the Early Engineers* (John Murray, 1874).

The Ship Canal's history is explored in Ernest Bosdin Leech, *History of the Manchester Ship Canal from its inception to its completion* (Sherratt & Hughes, 1907), David E. Owen, *The Manchester Ship Canal* (Manchester University Press, 1983), D.A. Farnie, *The Manchester Ship Canal and the rise of the Port of Manchester, 1894–1975* (Manchester University Press, 1980) and Chris Makepeace, *The Manchester Ship Canal* (Hendon Publishing Co., 1983).

MCL(M) has a collection of merchant ships' agreements, crew lists and official log books relating to ships registered at the port of Manchester from the opening of the Ship Canal in 1894 to 1913 (M110). CCALS holds deposited plans for the Manchester Ship Canal, Bridgewater Canal (QDN5), Mersey & Irwell Navigation (QDN3), etc.

CANAL ARCHIVES AND RECORDS

TNA hold the largest collection of canal company records, including those later taken over by railway companies, such as the Manchester Bolton and Bury Navigation and Railway (RAIL 458). Some canal company and British Waterways Board collections are held locally. Only a brief summary can be given here; use TNA Discovery, GMLives and the Waterways Archive online catalogues to explore the subject further.

The Bridgewater Canal Trust and Bridgewater Estates

The Canal Duke was childless. After his death in 1803 the estates were split; the northern estates, including the canal and industrial undertakings, passed to his nephew George Leveson Gower (later the 1st Duke of Sutherland). However, the Duke's canal and businesses were vested in a trust in such a fashion that the heir could not control them. The Bridgewater Trust now administered the old Duke's estate, and the heir received the income from it. In 1847 the Bridgewater Trustees bought the old Duke's rival, the Mersey & Irwell Navigation Company.

The 3rd Duke of Bridgewater also made sure that the estates were vested in a trust after his death. However, early in the twentieth century, after the 4th Earl of Ellesmere gained control of the estates, they were sold off to a group of Lancashire businessmen, Bridgewater Estates Ltd.

The huge Duke of Bridgewater Archive at UoS includes family papers and correspondence, maps and plans, etc. relating to the canal's construction (DBA). Salford University also holds the Bridgewater Estates archive from the 1890s to the 1960s (BEA). The archive relates to the administration of the estates, including collieries and property. A card catalogue is available.

SCA holds the Bridgewater Trust's enormous archives dating from the early fifteenth to the late nineteenth centuries (BW). The archive is divided into several series: estate administration and management (BW/A); estate finance (BW/F); manorial records (BW/M); and deeds of title (BW/T). Records of employees including wages, pensions and apprenticeship indentures are in BW/A/5. SCA also holds an account book for the Bridgewater Canal and other enterprises, 1770–1.

Other Canals

MCL(G) has several canal collections. The Manchester Ship Canal archive, 1884–1963 includes minute books, financial records, accident registers, cash books, etc. (B10). The Rochdale Canal archive, 1790–1963 includes minute books, ledgers, journals, cash books, share records, letter books, etc. (B2). The Mersey & Irwell Navigation/Bridgewater Canal records, 1779–1973 include minute books, engineer reports, toll traffic, share registers, staff records, etc. (M300). See the previous section for more archival materials relating to the Bridgewater Canal.

Canal companies employed lots of different workers: boatmen, engineers, clerks, toll clerks, boatmen, blacksmiths, navvies and so on, and these may be mentioned in minute books, wage books, staff ledgers, pension books, rent rolls, etc.

'Health registers' are very helpful for information on canal boat families. Following the Canal Boats Acts of 1877 and 1884, local authorities kept registers of canal boats. Sanitary inspectors checked the boats regularly to ensure they were not overcrowded and were clean. These records include owners' addresses; the inspectors' journals noted how many adults and children were on each boat. The health registers are sometimes catalogued as 'registers of canal boats and barges'. For example, Manchester City Council inspected boats on local canals and MCL(M) holds health records, 1909–72 (M487). The Waterways Archive (see below) holds some health registers and databases of registers.

Chetham's Library has a good collection of books and pamphlets relating to canals and railways; the Mullineux Photographic Archive includes images of the Bridgewater Canal and Ship Canal.

THE WATERWAYS ARCHIVE AT ELLESMERE PORT

The Waterways Archive at Ellesmere Port holds hundreds of documents, e.g. some relating to boats owned by the Manchester Ship Canal Company, company records, staff records and historic photos of canal boats and workers. It has a reference library, and a research service is available. You can visit the archive in person, or explore its collections online, http://collections.canalrivertrust.org.uk/home.

The Virtual Waterways Archive Catalogue gives the location of British Waterways and early canal company records in fifteen partner repositories. (NB Some archive addresses, and hyperlinks on this website are out of date) www.virtualwaterways.co.uk/search_quick. php. The website also has an introduction to researching family history on the waterways, www.virtualwaterways.co.uk/Family_History_ introduction. html.

THE RAILWAY AGE

Canal transport was subject to delays, too, especially in the winter months if the waterways froze, and the birth of the railways was the next milestone in the transport revolution.

The Bolton and Leigh Railway (1828) was the first in the Manchester region. It linked the Manchester, Bolton and Bury Canal to the Leeds and Liverpool Canal at Leigh and from there to the port of Liverpool. It was financed by local businessmen with the aim of transporting coal, stone, slate and other heavy goods.

The opening of the Liverpool and Manchester Railway on 15 September 1830 was an immense technical triumph – but the impetus for this revolutionary project did not come from Manchester. It was a group of Liverpool businessmen who funded the railway, and fought tooth and nail against vested canal interests. The construction of the railway, which cost over £1 million, was a huge challenge. The most serious obstacle it faced was the 12 square miles of Chat Moss, an ancient peat bog. Engineer George Stephenson solved the problem by 'floating' the railway across the Moss.

Trials were held at Rainhill on 6 October 1829 to discover which locomotive was the fastest and most reliable; Robert Stephenson's

Iron railway viaduct, Manchester. Illustrated London News, *11 January 1851.*
This cast-iron railway viaduct served the joint station of the LNWR and the
Manchester, Sheffield and Lincolnshire Railway (viewed from Store Street).
(Author's collection)

Rocket won the day's honours. Unfortunately, the *Rocket* was also
involved in the first ever railway accident on the Liverpool and
Manchester Railway's opening day. William Huskisson, MP for
Liverpool, died from his injuries after falling under the *Rocket*'s wheels.

   The great reduction in travel times afforded by the railways made
Manchester even more attractive as an industrial hub linking many
other parts of the country. After the Grand Junction Railway linked with
the Liverpool and Manchester in the late 1830s, passengers could travel
to London via Birmingham. The Manchester and Leeds Railway (1839)
linked Cottonopolis with Yorkshire's great woollen districts. The crossing
of the Pennines, which meant constructing the Summit Tunnel, was
another of George Stephenson's great technical achievements. This line
later became part of the Lancashire and Yorkshire Railway. In 1848
several railways amalgamated to form the London and North Western
Railway (LNWR).

There was great rivalry and competition between various railways to link Manchester with the rest of Britain. Unfortunately, there was very little cooperation between the railway companies, so by the late nineteenth century, Manchester had four railway termini in different parts of the city: Exchange Station, Hunt's Bank (later Victoria), Store Street (later London Road, then Piccadilly) and Central Station (Cheshire Lines Committee) – now the Manchester Central venue. This multiplicity of lines was decidedly inconvenient for passengers who needed to switch services. The former Liverpool Road station (the terminus of the Liverpool and Manchester Railway), which closed in 1844, now forms part of the Museum of Science and Industry.

The railways brought many benefits to Manchester folk as well as boosting the region's industry, manufacturing and distribution. Perishable goods could now reach the town centre while still fresh, and it was easier for ordinary workers to visit places like the seaside. For the growth of the food, drink and grocery trade, with maps and statistics, see W.A. Armstrong and P. Scola (eds) and Roger Scola, *Feeding the Victorian City: The Food Supply of Manchester 1770–1870* (Manchester University Press, 1992).

The company histories of the region's railways are extremely complex and beyond the scope of this work. In 1923, most British railways amalgamated into the 'Big Four': the Great Western Railway (GWR), the London, Midland and Scottish (LMS), London and North Eastern (LNER) and Southern Railway (SR). Then on 1 January 1948, British Railways was created when the rail system was nationalized.

Railway Sources

TNA has hundreds of collections on railway companies from the mid-1820s until 1947. Use TNA Discovery to search for staff registers, salary registers (for office staff), apprenticeship indentures, personnel and pension records. TNA's British Transport Historical Records (BTHR) collection has almost 150 record series, including staff records. TNA has a guide to researching rail staff before and after nationalization, www.nationalarchives.gov.uk/help-with-your-research/research-guides /railway-workers/.

MCL(M) holds British Rail plans, 1847–1924: M93. MCL(G) holds records relating to British Rail property (BRB); staff records and plans for the Great Central Railway (GCR); and British Rail plans, 1829–1972:

A19. CCALS holds records of British Rail London Midland and Western Regions, and predecessor companies, *c.*1838–1983 (NPR).

MCC libraries hold many different titles relating to railways in the region. See Paul Shannon and John Hillmer, *British Railways Past and Present. No. 41, Manchester and South Lancashire* (Wadenhoe, 2003); M.D. Greville, *Chronology of the Railways of Manchester* (Railway and Canal Historical Society, 1973); and William Harrison, *A history of the Manchester railways (1882)* (2nd edn) (LCAS, 1967).

For family history help, see David T. Hawkings, *Railway Ancestors* (History Press, 2008); Di Drummond, *Tracing Your Railway Ancestors* (Pen & Sword, 2010); and Frank Hardy, *My Ancestor Was A Railway Worker* (Society of Genealogists, 2009). Ancestry's collection of UK Railway Employment Records, 1833–1956 includes staff registers for the LNWR.

ACTS OF PARLIAMENT AND BLUE BOOKS

Before a company wanted to build a canal, railway or major road an Act of Parliament was required. If a proposed canal or railway affected other transport companies in the area, which meant they faced a potential loss of income, they sent petitions to Parliament against the scheme. Sometimes parliamentary committees were set up which took detailed witness statements from engineers and other interested parties.

Parliament ordered investigations into mining, the silk industry, hand-loom weaving, child labour, steel and many other trades and manufactures. These 'Blue Books', comprising 'sessional papers' and 'Command' papers, were ordered to be printed by the Houses of Parliament. Catalogues and indexes are available. Reports from the investigatory committees often include interviews with workers, managers and factory owners.

MCL has copies of the Irish University Press reprints of British Parliamentary papers (via the search room). You can access digital images of parliamentary papers in TNA's reading rooms at Kew. The Parliamentary Archives holds copies of parliamentary papers, Command papers, committee reports and minutes of evidence, www.parliament.uk/business/publications/parliamentary-archives/, and www.parliament.uk/about/how/publications/records/. Some Command papers and factory inspectors' reports are available free on Google Books, http://books.google.com.

FURTHER READING

Albert, William, *The Turnpike Road System in England 1663–1840*, Cambridge University Press, 1972

Aldcroft, Derek and Freeman, Michael, *Transport in the Industrial Revolution*, Manchester University Press, 1983

Ashmore, Owen, *The Industrial Archaeology of North-West England*, Chetham Society Third Series No. 29, Manchester University Press, 1982

Boughey, Joseph and Hadfield, Charles, *British Canals: The Standard History*, Tempus Publishing, 2008

Carter, C.F. (ed.), *Manchester And Its Region*, BAAS, Manchester University Press, 1962

De Salis, Henry, *Bradshaw's Canals and Navigable Rivers of England and Wales (1904)*, David & Charles, 1969

Gibson, Keith, *Pennine Pioneer: The History of the Rochdale Canal*, History Press, 2004

Keaveney, E. and Brown, D.L., *The Ashton Canal*, Keaveney & Brown, 1974

Owen, David, *Canals To Manchester*, Manchester University Press, 1987

Paget-Tomlinson, Edward, *Illustrated History of Canal & River Navigations*, Landmark Countryside Collection, 2006

Smiles, Samuel, *Lives of the Engineers: Brindley and the Early Engineers*, John Murray, 1874

Smiles, Samuel, *Lives of the Engineers: History of Roads*, John Murray, 1874

Webb, Sidney and Beatrice, *History of Local Government: The Story of the King's Highway*, Longmans, Green & Co., 1913

Wilkes, Sue, *Tracing Your Canal Ancestors*, Pen & Sword, 2011

Chapter 4

MADE IN MANCHESTER

COTTON AND TEXTILES

Manchester became synonymous with the cotton industry. But in medieval times, the town was known for its woollen and linen manufactures. Tradition has it that Edward II invited skilled Flemish weavers to settle in northwest England during the 1330s. Although the term Manchester 'cottons' was in use as early as the sixteenth century, these 'cottons' were made of wool.

By the early 1640s the area's textile industries were firmly established. Cotton yarn (imported via Ireland) was woven with linen yarn made from flax to make sturdy 'fustian' cloth.

Families like the Chethams, Mosleys and Tippings became very wealthy buying and selling woollen cloths, linens, cotton yarn and fustians. The wholesalers and master-manufacturers of Manchester became famous. As these 'Manchester men' became richer they built fine homes and large warehouses for their goods.

In the early 1700s pretty, light, all-cotton calicoes imported from India and the East threatened to wipe out the woollen trade. An Act of 1721 banned the wearing of, weaving or selling of any printed all-cotton 'stuffs' or 'calicoes', whether imported or made in Britain. However, 'fustians' were exempted. Woollen and worsted weavers petitioned Parliament to ban fustians, too, but the 'Manchester Act' of 1736 upheld the exemption. All-cotton printed goods remained banned, however.

During the 1740s, Manchester merchants bought the warps and raw cotton and gave it to weavers who worked in their own homes. The raw cotton was carded, and the fibres were straightened to form a long, fluffy 'roving'. The rovings were spun into yarn, then the yarn was wound onto bobbins and finally woven into cloth on a loom.

John Kay's flying shuttle (1733) made hand-weaving easier. Then several key inventions speeded up first the spinning, then weaving of cotton. Lewis Paul and John Wyatt had the idea of thinning out cotton fibre using rollers, and James Hargreaves' machine, the 'spinning jenny', patented in 1770, revolutionized spinning. Preston barber Richard Arkwright built on the work of Lewis Paul and Thomas Highs and created a spinning machine called a 'water-frame'.

Arkwright successfully petitioned Parliament to get the ban on all-cotton cloths repealed in 1774, which gave a huge boost to the cotton industry. Then Samuel Crompton's spinning 'mule' (1779) made strong yarn fine enough for weaving all-cotton cloth (calico) and delicate muslin. The big breakthrough for weaving came when Edmund Cartwright patented a powered loom in 1785. However, because handwoven cloth was of better quality than machine-made fabric, thousands of weavers still worked at home on hand looms. But during the nineteenth century, their wages went into inexorable decline as power loom weaving became more widespread.

As spinning jennies and mules became larger and more complex, manufacturers built factories to house them. Mule spinning was the province of men; women and young people tended power looms. Small children worked as 'piecers', i.e. they joined together broken threads on the spinning machines.

One of the earliest factories in Manchester may have been Mr Gartside's weaving establishment, opened in 1765. By the 1780s there were two mills in Manchester; Richard Arkwright and partners had one near Angel Meadow, and Mr Thackeray had one at Granby Row.

The first factories were water-powered and built by fast-flowing streams. The advent of steam power meant that factories could now be built wherever coal was plentiful. One of the first manufacturers to use steam to power the mill machinery was Peter Drinkwater, who built a cotton spinning mill in Manchester in 1789. Cotton factories and their contents were highly combustible, and Philips and Lee built the first 'fireproof' mill in the Manchester area (with cast-iron beams) in 1801. This mill, on Chapel Street in Salford, was also the first factory in Britain to be lit by gas.

By 1816, Manchester contained 43 working mills; the largest employer was McConnel & Kennedy, with over 1,000 workers. These early factories worked day and night. Manufacturers like William Douglas of Pendleton relied on pauper apprentice workers, some from as far away as London. Douglas' mill at Pendleton was known to locals as the 'Cripples Factory' because of the inhumane way his child workers were treated. The Health and Morals of Apprentices Act of 1802 limited workhouse children's shifts in cotton mills to 12 hours daily.

Later, the 1833 Factory Act ended night work for all children under 18 in all textile mills except lace factories. This Act established the factory inspectorate, and more stringent legislation was adopted throughout the nineteenth century. The 1847 Factory Act made school attendance compulsory for factory children for a set number of hours per week ('half-timers') and they were not permitted to work without a school attendance certificate signed by a teacher. Inspectors visited factories and prosecuted firms for breaches of the Factory Act. Firms kept statutory records of children and young persons.

Self-acting mule 'on Sharp & Robert's principle' constructed by P. Macgregor, Manchester (possibly at the Falcon Works on Poland Street). Popular Encyclopedia *(Blackie & Son, c.1862), Vol. III. (Author's collection)*

The runaway success of the cotton industry led Manchester to become a symbol of the trade: 'Cottonopolis'. In the 1760s, Britain imported fewer than 4 million lb of cotton. By 1787, this had increased to over 23 million lb and continued to increase. In 1849 cotton imports had reached 754 million lb. Manchester was the grand centre of its manufacture, and finished cotton exports were worth £27 million.

The trade received a setback when the American Civil War virtually put an end to imports of cotton from the slave plantations in the early 1860s. Despite the great distress in Lancashire mills (the 'cotton famine'), many Manchester folk supported the fight to end slavery. MLIA has an online guide to its resources on Manchester and the slave trade, http://bit.ly/2hV8gPQ.

As well as cotton, woollens, worsted, silk, flannel, linen and velvets were made in the area, and there were thriving bleaching, printing and dyeing factories. Thomas Hoyle's Mayfield dyeing and printing works employed over 200 workers in the 1830s, including over 40 children.

The Manchester Statistical Society reported in 1837–8 that Manchester had 5,272 cotton spinning and weaving mills powered by steam; Salford had 761 steam-powered cotton mills. Manchester had 756 bleaching, dyeing and print works powered by steam, and Salford had 521 establishments. Machine manufacturers, foundries, silk mills, breweries, saw mills, collieries and chemical works in the area were also steam-powered.

By late Victorian times, there was little cotton manufacture in Manchester city centre, but it remained the UK's centre for cotton yarn and cloth sales until foreign competition forced the industry into decline during the twentieth century. See *The Decline of the Cotton and Coal Mining Industries of Lancashire* (Lancashire and Merseyside Industrial Development Association, 1967) and Terry Wyke and Nigel Rudyard's *Cotton: A Select Bibliography on Cotton in North-West England*, Bibliography of North West England (Manchester, 1997).

Wyke and Rudyard's *Bibliography* is especially useful because hundreds of works have been written on the cotton industry. For Manchester's role, see, for example, George W. Daniels, *The Early English Cotton Industry* (Manchester University Press, 1920); R.S. Fitton, *The Arkwrights: Spinners of Fortune* (Manchester University Press, 1989); Mike Williams and D.A. Farnie, *Cotton Mills in Greater Manchester* (Royal Commission on Historical Monuments, 1992); and R. Lloyd-Jones and

The Irwell at Ordsall, Salford; Worrall's dye works is on the right. Illustration by H.E. Tidmarsh, Manchester Old and New *(Cassell & Co., c.1894), Vol. III. (Author's collection)*

M.J. Lewis, *Manchester and the Age of the Factory* (Croom Helm, 1988).

The MLFHS website has a database of names and address for over 1,000 reed-makers in northwest England, www.mlfhs.org.uk/data /reedmakers.pdf (a reed forms part of a hand loom). The society's members can also access a database of McConnel & Kennedy mill workers mentioned in the 1833 Factory Commission (these lists of employees were compiled in 1818–19).

COAL MINING

The enormous south Lancashire coal field played a major role in Manchester and Salford becoming industrial hubs. Small-scale mining took place during medieval times in shallow 'drift' or 'bell' pits. Manchester was plentifully supplied with coal from pits in Pendleton, Pendlebury and Worsley, and further afield, from Wigan collieries.

Men worked as coal 'getters' (hewing the ore). Over time, the coal seams near the surface became worked out, so deeper and deeper shafts were sunk. One shaft at Pendleton in the 1830s was 500yd deep, which was extremely deep for that era. Manchester historian James Wheeler estimated that 2,000 miners worked in the area in 1835, earning between 3s. 6d. and 7s 6d. per day (a good wage).

The seams in Lancashire pits were notoriously narrow, and child labour was common. Children as young as 4 worked as 'trappers', opening and closing ventilation doors as miners passed with loaded tubs of coal. Women, boys and girls were 'drawers', harnessed to coal wagons with a belt and chain. They dragged, pushed and pulled incredibly heavy loads from the coal face to the main shaft. Following a shocking report on working conditions in 1842, all females and boys under 10 were banned from underground work, but the law was widely flouted.

People also worked at the pit brow: winding engine men (engineers), joiners, wheelwrights, banksmen, blacksmiths (for the pit ponies), labourers, etc. Pit-brow lasses screened, picked over and cleaned the coal or shovelled it into railway wagons.

Mining was dangerous work. Workers died in rock falls, explosions from firedamp or chokedamp, waggon accidents and suffered from heart and lung diseases. The miners paid into sick and burial clubs, and formed trade unions, so their families would have help if they were unable to work.

In 1859, the mines inspector Joseph Dickinson reported 138 mining deaths in the Manchester district (which covered north and east Lancashire). He highlighted several accidents at the collieries owned by the Knowles family (*Reports of the Inspectors of Mines . . . to December 1859*, Vol. XXIII, [2740], 1860). Seven people, colliers and drawers, died in one incident on 4 January 1859 at Agecroft colliery while ascending the pit. The cage they were travelling in got caught in the top of the winding pulley and the men and boys were flung down the mine shaft. There was another major disaster at the Clifton Hall pit in June 1885, when nearly 180 people perished; some were laid to rest in Weaste Cemetery.

Manchester Collieries Ltd (1929) was an amalgamation of several mining firms, including Andrew Knowles and Sons, and Bridgewater Collieries Ltd. The whole mining industry, including local firms, was fully nationalized in 1947 when the National Coal Board was formed.

New mines were being sunk as late as the 1950s, when Agecroft colliery was surveyed and re-opened. But pits began to close as the old seams were exhausted, and cheap foreign imports made mining uneconomic. No working mines are now left in Lancashire.

The National Coal Board collection at LA (NC) covers 1495–1964 and includes accident books, Lancashire and Cheshire miners' welfare committee, colliery doctors' certificates, etc. The collection includes the records of Andrew Knowles and Sons Ltd (NCKn), Bridgewater Collieries Ltd (NCBw) and Manchester Collieries Ltd (NCMc) – accounts, wages, pension fund, benevolent fund, rentals, etc.

LA also holds the collection formerly belonging to the Salford Museum of Mining (later known as the Lancashire Coal Mining Museum) which was once at Buile Hill Park, Salford. The collection (NC/acc9529) includes colliery records, papers of mining union branches, colliery plans, machinery drawings and research papers.

SCA's Bridgewater Estates collection includes mining (e.g. at Worsley and Hulton) in the manorial archives (BW/M) and estate administration records (BW/A and BW/T). Mining engineers and surveyors Joseph Jackson & Co.'s records at SCA include surveys, maps and plans from the early nineteenth century to *c*.1940 (U65).

TNA has many collections relating to mining including pits owned by the Duchy of Lancaster, the mining inspectorate, strikes (including the 1984 stoppage), wartime, etc. (NB there are no staff records at Kew.) The website has a guide to exploring the industry, www.national archives.gov.uk/help-with-your-research/research-guides/mines-mining. The COAL series includes photos of collieries in the Greater Manchester area in the 1930s (COAL 80).

For advice on finding mining ancestors, see David Tonks, *My Ancestor Was A Coalminer* (Society of Genealogists, 2003) and Brian Elliott, *Tracing Your Coalmining Ancestors* (Pen & Sword, 2015).

For Salford coal mining, see Geoff Preece, *Coalmining In Salford* (City of Salford Cultural Service, 1981). The Irwell Valley Mining Project is dedicated to raising awareness of Salford's coal-mining history, and its website has photos and videos, www.ivmp.org.uk. See Paul Kelly, *The Last Pit in the Valley* (Unity Publishing, 2013).

• Ian Winstanley's former Coal Mining History Resource Centre website is now defunct but archived at http://bit.ly/2frq7kg. This database of UK mining deaths and injuries is also available on Ancestry, http://bit.ly/2dYSXrj.

• MLIA has a Flickr page dedicated to Bradford Pit, http://bit.ly/1Yg6bPj.
• The Durham Mining Museum website lists colliery disasters and deaths (including some in Lancashire pits), with name indexes, www.dmm.org.uk/mindex.htm.

ENGINEERING, CHEMICAL AND OTHER INDUSTRIES

The Manchester area was also famous for electrical engineering, the chemical industry and 'heavy' industries, such as metal-working, textile machinery and locomotive manufacture. During the 1820s, the Mather family set up an iron-founding business in Salford. In the 1850s this firm joined forces with the Platt family, and Mather & Platt went on to become a major manufacturer of textile machinery. Later in the century, the firm moved into electrical engineering.

Scotsman James Nasmyth (1808–90) was one of the most famous engineers of his day. In his early twenties, he worked for the renowned engineer Henry Maudsley in London, before setting up his own business at Dale Street in Manchester. In 1839, he founded the Bridgewater Foundry at Patricroft, Eccles, and three years later the first steam hammer in Britain was forged at this works.

See James Nasmyth and Samuel Smiles (ed.), *James Nasmyth Engineer: An Autobiography* (John Murray, 1883); John A. Cantrell, *James Nasmyth and the Bridgewater Foundry* (Manchester University Press, 1986) and *Nasmyth, Wilson & Co.: Patricroft Locomotive Builders* (History Press, 2005) by the same author.

SCA holds records for Nasmyth, Wilson & Co. (iron-founders, locomotive, hydraulic and general engineers), 1836–1985 including letter books, day books, order books, sales books, record of locomotives sold, production notes, plans and research papers (U268, U269). SCA has a collection of notebooks made by Nathan Walker (a worker at the factory) relating to locomotives and boilers made at Nasmyth's works from 1875–1939 (U49). SCA also has a collection of Nasmyth's correspondence (U312, U313).

Sir Joseph Whitworth (1803–87), another famous engineer, had a works at Chorlton Street, Manchester which made machine tools, guns and cannon. Among Whitworth's inventions were a self-acting planing machine and a micrometer capable of measuring a thickness of one-ten-thousandth of an inch; he also created a standard system of screw

James Nasmyth An etching by Paul Rajon after the portrait by George Reid, from James Nasmyth, Engineer *(John Murray, 1883). (Nigel Wilkes collection)*

The Bridgewater Foundry, Patricroft. From a painting by Alexander Nasmyth. James Nasmyth, Engineer *(John Murray, 1883). (Nigel Wilkes collection)*

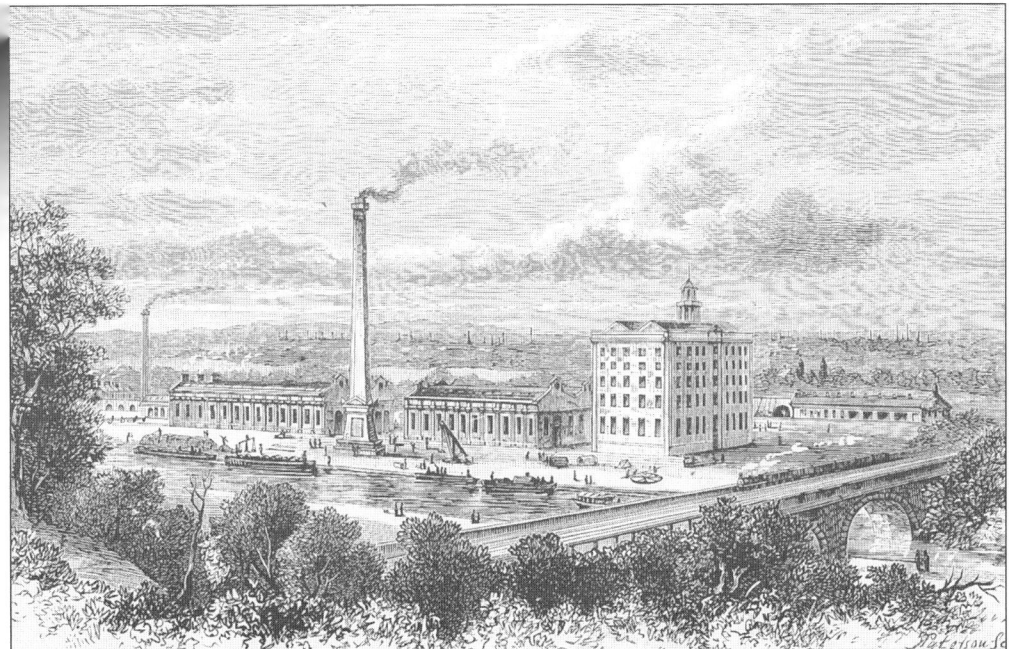

thread sizes. Innovations like these were vital for the precision machine engineering needed to keep Lancashire's mills and factories humming. MCL(M) holds a bills ledger for Armstrong, Whitworth & Co.'s Openshaw works (MISC/1091).

William Fairbairn had a huge works on Canal Street in Ancoats which made boilers and bridges. Platt Brothers made textile machinery at Oldham; this firm also had its own forges, rolling mills and brick works. Sharp, Roberts & Co.'s world-famous Atlas Works, founded in the late 1820s in Manchester, made locomotive engines.

At Gorton, Beyer-Peacock began manufacturing locomotives in the 1850s, the Ashbury Railway Carriage Company made railway carriages and waggons, and Crossley Brothers made engines and pumps. Northeast Manchester was home to a thriving chemical industry; carbolic acid, sulphuric acid and synthetic dyes were just some of the products made locally.

The Manchester Ship Canal inspired Britain's first purpose-built industrial estate. In 1896 Trafford Park, ancestral home of the de Trafford family, was sold to a developer. Trafford Hall was converted into a hotel, and a housing estate was constructed for workers. The Trafford Park Estates Co. built a railway link to the Ship Canal and before long major companies such as British Westinghouse Electrical and Manufacturing Company (later Metropolitan-Vickers or 'MetroVicks') and W.T. Glover built factories on the new industrial estate. Flour mills, iron works, oil refineries, timber works and lard refineries also sprang up. Metropolitan-Vickers manufactured Lancaster bombers for A.V. Roe and Co. (AVRO) during the Second World War. MCL(G) has a collection of publicity material printed for the Trafford Park Development Corporation (TPDC).

BUSES, TRAMS AND MOTOR VEHICLES

Until the early nineteenth century, Manchester merchants lived a short walk from their place of business. They gradually abandoned the town centre for the suburbs, however. In 1824 the toll-bar keeper at Pendleton, John Greenwood, saw a business opportunity and set up an omnibus service from Pendleton to Market Street in Manchester. (This may have been the earliest bus service in the UK.) By the mid-1850s Greenwood and his family ran over sixty buses, and in 1865 he founded the Manchester Carriage Co.

Greenwood also constructed a novel form of tramway in Salford (*c*.1860), which was abandoned a few years later, perhaps because of reliability problems. Meanwhile, in Manchester in 1875, the corporation gained powers to lay tram lines in the city. A private company, the Manchester Carriage and Tramways Company, leased the right to run the trams, which carried passengers between the two towns. This company was an amalgam of the Manchester Carriage Co. and the Manchester Suburban Tramways Company. These trams were still horse-drawn.

Over the years a complex network of tramways grew up. Some local companies flirted briefly with steam trams, but they did not catch on, and in 1901 Manchester Corporation and Salford Corporation began running their first electric tram services. Sadly, this cheap, reliable mode of transport was superseded by motor vehicles, and the tram lines began to disappear during the Second World War. Ironically, cars are no longer seen as an asset in city centres, and trams returned to Manchester when the Metrolink opened in 1992.

MCL(M) holds records for Manchester Corporation Transport, 1873–1969 (M29) and Salford Corporation Transport Department, 1861–1948 (M125); these series include tramways and trolleybuses. The records for the Manchester Branch of the Transport and General Workers' Union, 1889–1970 held at MCL(M) include newspaper cuttings and photos (M86). Tameside Local Studies and Archives holds some material relating to Manchester Corporation Tramways including newspaper cuttings (ref. 0351).

See Chris Heaps and Michael Eyre, *Manchester and Salford: A Century of Municipal Transport (Glory Days)* (Ian Allan Publishing, 2001); Ted Gray and Arthur Kirby, *Manchester trams: a pictorial history of the tramways of Manchester* (Manchester Memories, 1995); Ian Yearsley and Philip Groves, *The Manchester Tramways* (Transport Publishing Company, 1991); Edward Gray, *Salford City Transport* (Transport Publishing Company, 1975); and Edward Gray, *The Tramways of Salford* (Manchester Transport Museum, 1967).

Manchester played a pioneering role in Britain's early motor industry, too. Belsize Motors, founded *c*.1901, had a factory in Clayton, and Crossley Brothers began making cars at Openshaw shortly afterwards. The latter firm set up a new company, Crossley Motors, which later moved to Gorton.

However, the industry's early promise hit the brakes when the Ford Motor Co., which had a factory at Trafford Park, moved away from the area in the late 1920s. (It returned during the Second World War to manufacture Merlin engines.)

Another successful manufacturer was Joseph Cockshoot & Co. Joseph founded a coach-building works in Manchester in the 1840s; the firm was renowned for the quality of its products. Early in the twentieth century, Cockshoot's began manufacturing bodies for motor cars; its customers included Rolls-Royce and Mercedes. During the Second World War, the firm manufactured parts for Britain's military aircraft.

MOSI holds the records of automobile engineering firm Joseph Cockshoot & Co. Ltd, 1867–1968, including financial papers, photographs and employee records (YA1970.36/MS0196), and automobile engineers H. & J. Quick, 1914–2000 (2008.10). The Modern Records Centre, Warwick holds records for Crossley Motors Ltd, 1910–66 (CRM) including minutes, share records and cash books; MOSI holds some photographs and parts lists (YA10.65).

See A.D. George, 'The Manchester Motor Industry 1900–1938', *Transport History* (9), 1978, pp. 217–22, and 'The Manchester Motor Industry 1900–1938: Further Notes', *Transport History* (10), 1979, pp. 171–5, by the same author. For the history of buses in the area, see *A Century of Motor Buses in Manchester* (Greater Manchester Transport Society, 2006).

The Greater Manchester Transport Museum

The museum has a collection of books on the area's transport history, as well as directories, yearbooks and commemorative brochures for bodies such as Manchester Corporation Transport Department and Salford City Transport, www.gmts.co.uk/documents.html. The museum also has a large photographic collection; over 300 photos are on Flickr, https://www.flickr.com/photos/gmts.

AIR TRAVEL

Two Manchester men, John Alcock and Alliott Verdon Roe, were aviation pioneers. Alcock and A.Whitten-Brown made the first transatlantic flight in 1919. Ten years earlier, Roe set up an aircraft manufacturing company with his brother: A.V. Roe and Co. Ltd (later known as AVRO). AVRO was bought by Crossley Motors Ltd in 1920.

In 1928 Manchester City Council decided it must take advantage of this exciting new form of transport, and founded Britain's first municipal airport. A temporary aerodrome was set up at Rackhouse, Wythenshawe. It was followed by Barton Aerodrome (now City Airport) which was licensed by the Air Ministry in 1920, but the first passenger flight did not take off until 1930. However, Barton was soon found unsuitable for the expected volume of traffic, and Ringway Airport opened eight years later.

See Brian R. Robinson, *Aviation in Manchester: A Short History* (Royal Aeronautical Society (Manchester Branch), 1977); R.A. Scholefield, 'Manchester's Early Airfields', Vol. 100, LCAS, 2004 and Viv Caruana, 'Manchester Airport: From Provincial Aerodrome to International Gateway' in the same volume.

MCL(M) holds the papers of R.A. Sorby, an aeronautical engineer who worked at AVRO during the 1950s (MISC/1258), and aircraft movement log books for Manchester Airport, 1958–87 (M332).

Museum of Science and Industry, Manchester

A visit to the museum's many galleries of machinery (some working) is a great way to explore the industrial development of northwest England, including the railways; it also has a large exhibition devoted to air and space technology. MOSI has an archive that you can explore by appointment. Archive holdings include materials for the Calico Printers Association, Electricity Council, Mather & Platt business records, Paterson Zochonis, Beyer, Peacock & Co., A.V. Roe & Co., 1910–63 including photographs; British Westinghouse and Metropolitan-Vickers, Ferranti, Linotype & Machinery Co. Ltd, factory records, company minute books, photographs, trade directories, textile samples and designs. http://msimanchester.org.uk/.

COMMERCE AND BANKING

Far more Manchester people were employed selling and distributing goods than in manufacturing them. The city was famous for its enormous warehouses such as S. and J. Watts' building on Portland Street. In the 1930s, 84,000 people worked in 'the distributive trades', as well as '30,000 each in the cotton and engineering industries, another 20,000 in tailoring, and 15,000 in six other trades, namely, building, electrical engineering, clothing, rubber, printing, and textile finishing' (*The City of Manchester: 1936* (Manchester Corporation, 1936)).

Smithfield Market, Manchester. The Queen's Empire *(Cassell & Co. Ltd, 1899).*
(Author's collection)

Royal Exchange, Manchester. Our Own Country *(Cassell & Co., n.d., c.1883),*
Vol. III. (Author's collection)

Manchester was also an important banking centre, and the Bank of England opened its own branch in the town in 1826. Benjamin Heywood and his sons founded a bank on Exchange Street in 1788; this firm later became Heywood Brothers & Co. In the 1870s it was bought by the Manchester and Salford Bank. See Leo H. Grindon, *Manchester Banks and Bankers* (Manchester, 1878) and George Chandler, *Four Centuries of Banking* (Batsford, 1968).

Early steam boilers were prone to exploding without warning, and textile factories were particularly bad fire risks. A specialist insurance industry grew up to serve the needs of the area's commercial and industrial community, and MCL(G) holds collections for the Boiler Insurance and Steam Power Co. Ltd, the National Vulcan Engineering and Insurance Group, and Vulcan Boiler and General Insurance Co. Ltd (B9). For information on fire-insurance records and their location, see David T. Hawkings, *Fire Insurance Records for Family and Local Historians* (Francis Boutle, 2003).

Manchester's first Exchange (1729) for commercial transactions was built in the market place by Sir Oswald Mosley. The first stone of the second Exchange was laid in 1806; its newsroom opened three years later, and a post office was added in 1839. As the railways brought more and more trade to Manchester, more space was needed and the Royal Exchange was rebuilt in the 1870s. After the First World War the building was greatly extended until the site covered nearly 2 acres. Although the Exchange was mainly devoted to the cotton industry, its members also dealt with banking, bleaching, coal, metals, chemicals, stock and share transactions, etc.

The town's first trading and manufacturing association was the Manchester Commercial Society (1794), which had over twenty members. By the 1930s Manchester Chamber of Commerce comprised over 2,300 leading firms, and it watched carefully over the city's interests at home and abroad.

The Chamber of Commerce records, 1794–1999 (M8 at MCL(M)) include annual reports and registers of members. The Local Studies Library at MCL has publications relating to Manchester Chamber of Commerce including Annual Reports (some on microfilm), lists of members, handbooks, memorandums and articles of association, and monthly reports. MCL(G) holds twentieth-century records for Eccles Chamber of Commerce (B.CCOM).

Barclays Group Archives, Wythenshawe

The archive serves the whole of Barclays Group. Only limited systematic name indexes are available for customers and employees, and searches can only be conducted if a researcher can show that an ancestor worked for or banked with one of its constituent banks. The archive has some records for the Lancashire and Yorkshire Bank, 1864–1970, the Mercantile Bank of Lancashire, 1890–1904, and the Union Bank of Manchester, 1836–1940. Records include 'signature books': lists of names of account holders (sometimes with addresses and occupations). The directors' minutes of these banks (and smaller constituent banks) also contain names of customers (personal and business). The archive also has staff appointments and retirement records.

A letter of introduction or ID is required to visit the archive; appointments must be made in advance. Management records have a 30-year closure rule; for customer records the closure is 100 years. https://www.archive.barclays.com/.

Royal Bank of Scotland Archives

This archive holds records for Heywood Brothers & Co. including partnership records, financial records and customer records (HB), and Williams Deacon's Bank (formerly the Manchester and Salford Bank) (WD), http://heritagearchives.rbs.com.

RESEARCHING WORKERS, COMPANIES, INDUSTRIES AND TRADES

It is beyond the scope of this work to give a full account of the growth of Manchester and Salford's many industries, and the reader is encouraged to explore the subject more thoroughly using the references given.

MCL(M) holds over 200 collections relating to local businesses and factories, including the English Sewing Cotton Co. Ltd (M127) and the Calico Printers' Association (M75 and M159). MCL(G) holds business records for over sixty organizations such as the Lancashire Cotton Corporation, 1921–70 (B/CTLD), Tootal Broadhurst Lee Co. Ltd (M461) and the Manchester and Salford Savings Bank, 1817–1978.

Use TNA Discovery, GMLives and the Archives Hub to find surviving company records such as minute books, financial accounts and correspondence. If the company you are researching is still extant,

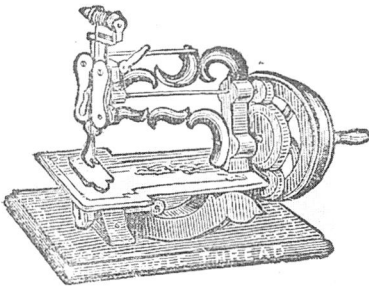

Advert for Mackenzie's Royal Sewing Machine Depot on Market Street. Manchester Historical Recorder (*John Heywood, Manchester, c.1875*). *(Author's collection)*

you may need to request access to its records. Solicitors' records may include correspondence with local companies. Quarter sessions papers may include insolvency papers for debtors (e.g. QJB at LA); bankruptcies were reported in newspapers and the *London Gazette*.

If your ancestor worked in a particular industry, apprentice indentures, wage books, trade-union records, staff and pension records are all useful sources. You can trace a company's progress through time using historical directories (see below) and the Companies Registration Office series at TNA; the website has an online guide, www. nationalarchives.gov.uk/help-with-your-research/research-guides/businesses/.

Grace's Guide is a free comprehensive directory of early industrial and manufacturing companies, many of which were in Manchester and Salford. It has brief company histories, with references and links to further information online, www.gracesguide.co.uk/Main_Page.

Trade and Commercial Directories and Telephone Directories
Historical and trade directories are vital for discovering addresses for local businesses, firms, industries, agents for canal, road and rail companies, schools, shops, etc. Early directories often include the names of local gentry, too. The earliest trade directory for the area of interest was Elizabeth Raffald's *Directory of Manchester and Salford*, first published in 1772. Mrs Raffald was the author of *The Experienced English Housekeeper*. In 1780 the third edition of the *Directory* was being sold from the Exchange Coffee-House for 1s: a modern reprint of the *Directory* is available. See G.H. Tupling, *Lancashire directories 1684–1957* (Manchester Joint Committee on the Lancashire Bibliography, 1968).

You can browse and search free online trade directories from the University of Leicester's Special Collections, dating from the 1760s to the early twentieth century, including Slater's and Pigot's publications, http://specialcollections.le.ac.uk/cdm/landingpage/collection/p16445coll4.

MCL (cabinet 12) has copies of street directories on microfilm for Manchester from the late eighteenth century until the 1960s, and for Lancashire from the early nineteenth century to the end of the First World War, http://bit.ly/2i55MBT. MLFHS has published a guide, *Commercial Directories In Manchester Central Library* (2004) (the 'Orange Book'). Online genealogy suppliers such as Ancestry and The Genealogist (http://www.thegenealogist.co.uk) have digitized copies of trade directories.

The first telephone directories appeared towards the end of the nineteenth century, but not many of these are extant. MCL has a collection of telephone directories and *Yellow Pages* from 1984 onwards; these can be viewed by appointment in the search room.

Apprenticeship Records

Apprenticeship indentures and agreements often contain family information. Until 1814, the Statute of Artificers and Apprentices (1563) made it compulsory for young people who were learning a 'craft, trade or mystery' to serve an apprenticeship first. An indenture was a legal document recording the terms of the apprenticeship; often a sum of money ('premium') was paid to the child's master to seal the bargain. After the Statute of Artificers was repealed, apprenticeships were no longer mandatory, but many trades kept them as a useful training method.

Under the Poor Laws, parish overseers apprenticed out children in their care who were orphans or whose parents were receiving parish relief. These children were apprenticed into textile mills (as mentioned earlier), coal mining, farm labour, the navy, fishing, chimney sweeping, etc. Girls were commonly apprenticed as domestic servants. Registers of parish apprentices and parish apprenticeship indentures can be found in parish overseers' records, parish vestry records and board of guardian records (see Chapter 5). Quarter sessions records (see Chapter 7) often include disputes about apprenticeships, for example, LA's quarter sessions collection include Manchester masters and apprentices.

MLIA's collection of apprenticeship records, 1700–1849 (available on Findmypast) includes over 600 indentures – mostly parish apprentices, but over 60 records are for private apprenticeships to tradesmen. For example, on 2 February 1723 Sarah Simmon of Penwortham was apprenticed to William Bowker, Dutch loom weaver at Manchester for three years.

From 1710–1811 tax was paid on apprenticeship premiums. These payments were recorded by the Commissioners of Stamps in the Apprenticeship Books at TNA (IR 1). Parish and charity apprenticeships were exempt from this tax. The IR 1 series is free to view on Ancestry. Each record includes the name of the child and their master, date of indenture, date when the tax was paid, the premium paid and length of apprenticeship.

Findmypast has an index to Metropolitan-Vickers apprenticeship records for electrical engineering apprentices and trainees at Trafford Park, 1902–34. The transcripts usually include name, address, dates of apprenticeship or training, type of apprenticeship, whether deceased by 1935, and if so cause of death, http://search.findmypast.co.uk/search-world-records/electrical-engineering-apprentices-and-trainees-1902-1 934. MLFHS members can also access this index via the society's website.

MADE IN GREATER MANCHESTER
This new blog is a partnership between Bolton Archives and Local Studies, Bury Archives and Local & Family History Service, Manchester Libraries, Information and Archives, Oldham Local Studies and Archives, Stockport Local Heritage Library, Tameside Local Studies and Archives, Trafford Local Studies, Rochdale Local Studies and Archives, Salford City Archives and Local History Library, and Wigan Archives and Local Studies. The partnership is creating an online catalogue of local business records, and new digital resources for business history. https://madeingm.wordpress.com/.

TRADING CONSEQUENCES
This online resource gives access to historical documents such as parliamentary papers relating to trade, industry and transport, for example, trading reports or select committee reports, http://tcqdev.edina.ac.uk/search/commodity/.

Search the database by commodity (e.g. cotton) or location. Unfortunately, the online documents can only be accessed via ProQuest, which is prohibitively expensive unless you can access it from an academic institution. However, since each search elicits the name of those parliamentary papers with relevant information, you can check if copies are available at MCL or the British Library, or the Parliamentary Archives.

FURTHER READING
Bates, Denise, *Pit Lasses: Women and Girls in Coalmining c.1800–1914*, Pen & Sword, 2012
Burton, Anthony, *The Miners*, Futura Publications, 1977

Challinor, Raymond, *The Lancashire and Cheshire Miners*, Frank Graham, 1972

Chapman, Sydney J., *The Lancashire Cotton Industry*, Manchester University Press, 1904

Clay, H. and Brady, K. (eds), *Manchester At Work: A Survey*, Sherratt & Hughes, 1929

Emm, Adele, *Tracing Your Trade and Craftsman Ancestors*, Pen & Sword, 2015

Farnie, Douglas A., *The English Cotton Industry and the World Market 1815–96*, Clarendon Press, 1979

Hayes, Geoffrey, *Collieries and their Railways in the Manchester Coalfields*, Landmark, 2004

Honeyman, Katrina, *Child Workers in England 1780–1820*, Ashgate Publishing Ltd, 2007

Hutchins, B.L. and Harrison, A., *A History of Factory Legislation*, Frank Cass & Co. Ltd, 1966

Orbell, John and Turton, Alison, *British Banking, A Guide to Historical Records*, Ashgate Publishing, 2001

Teasdale, V., *Tracing Your Textile Ancestors*, Pen & Sword, 2009

Timmins, Geoffrey, *The Last Shift: the Decline of Handloom Weaving in Nineteenth Century Lancashire*, Manchester University Press, 1993

Timmins, Geoffrey, *Made in Lancashire: A History of Regional Industrialization*, Manchester University Press, 1998

Turnbull, G., *History of the Calico-Printing Industry of Great Britain*, John Sherratt & Sons, 1951

Wadsworth, Alfred P. and Mann, Julia de Lacy, *The Cotton Trade and Industrial Lancashire 1600–1780*, Manchester University Press, 1931

Wilkes, Sue, *Narrow Windows, Narrow Lives: The Industrial Revolution in Manchester*, History Press, 2008

Wilkes, Sue, *The Children History Forgot*, Robert Hale, 2011

Chapter 5

LOCAL GOVERNMENT AND THE POOR

MANCHESTER AND SALFORD POLICE COMMISSIONERS

Prior to their incorporation, Manchester and Salford were controlled by the ancient manorial courts and their officers, the borough-reeve and constables (see Chapter 7). The parish authorities (churchwardens and overseers) were responsible for poor relief (see below) and maintaining the highways.

The towns' police commissioners were responsible for street cleaning, lighting and the night watch. In 1765 a Cleansing and Lighting Committee was set up for Manchester and Salford, but this body appears to have made little progress in sanitary reform. Following the Manchester and Salford Police Act (1792), the towns were divided into eight districts, each with fifteen elected commissioners. The 120 police commissioners were responsible for paving, lighting, sewerage, watching and cleaning, so in many respects they took over the manorial courts' functions. The introduction of gas lighting (1807) was one of the Manchester and Salford police commissioners' success stories; a gas works was erected ten years later.

Townships like Baguley and Chorlton-upon-Medlock administered themselves before they became part of Manchester; dates of incorporation and series references for each township are noted in Table 3 opposite. The individual township series typically include minute books; constables' accounts; Poor Law records; parish overseers' records; highway surveyors' records; rate books; valuation lists; maps and plans, etc.

Table 3: Manchester Township Records at MCL(M)

District	Dates Covered	Series Ref
Ardwick	1821–1909	M10/1
Baguley Manor and Township	1705–1931	M10/2
Beswick	1859–96	M10/3
Blackley	1822–95	M10/4
Bradford	1859–97	M10/5
Burnage	1861–1901	M10/6
Cheetham	1693–1895	M10/7
Chorlton-cum-Hardy	1839–1911	M10/8
Chorlton-upon-Medlock	1718–1895	M10/9
Clayton	1875–1921	M10/10
Crumpsall	1841–95	M10/11
Didsbury	1847–1911	M10/12
Etchells Manor and Township	1569–1931	M10/20
Gorton	1824–1911	M10/13
Harpurhey	1842–95	M10/14
Hulme	1761–1901	M10/15
Levenshulme	1810–1909	M10/16
Manchester	1752–1952	M9
Moston	1838–95	M10/18
Moss Side	1841–1901	M10/17
Newton	1819–1904	M10/19
Northenden Manor and Township	1620–1931	M10/21
Openshaw	1838–95	M10/22
Rusholme	1768–1896	M10/23
Withington	1850–1915	M10/24

Not all of the early records for the Manchester and Salford Police Commissioners appear to have survived. However, the Manchester township collection at MCL(M) includes the police commissioners' minute books, 1797–1840; minute books for the Watch, Nuisance and Hackney Coach Committee papers; and minute books for the Lamp, Scavenging and Main Sewer Committee (M9). See Chapter 7 for the borough-reeve's and constables' papers.

'New Town Hall, Manchester'. Our Own Country (Cassell & Co., n.d., c.1883), Vol. III. (Author's collection)

MANCHESTER CORPORATION AND CITY COUNCIL

Early in Queen Victoria's reign, it had become clear to Manchester's merchants, businessmen and scientists that the arcane medieval machinery by which the town was governed was no longer fit for purpose. As we shall see later, the town's streets were filthy and its houses were overcrowded, unsanitary and unfit for human habitation.

The Manchester and Salford police commissioners failed to grapple with the scale of the problems caused by the towns' growing populations, nor could they cope with any major problems of law and order. The police commissioners could not raise enough money to perform their functions properly, and local ratepayers were reluctant to pay for better services.

Calico printers Richard Cobden and William Neild, banker Sir Benjamin Heywood, industrialist Thomas Potter and others were instrumental in the fight to gain Manchester a charter of incorporation. Manchester became a borough in 1838, and the first Borough Council met on 16 December 1838; Thomas Potter was the first mayor.

Unfortunately, the 'old guard' who formerly ran the town did not want to give up their privileges without a fight. The police commissioners refused to allow the new council to use the town hall (founded in 1822 on the Cross Street corner of King Street). Instead, the council held its meetings at the York Hotel in King Street. In 1842 Parliament confirmed Manchester's charter and the town was granted its own coat of arms.

However, the corporation still did not have the full legal powers it needed to run Manchester. On 24 March 1845 the council resolved to buy the manorial rights from Sir Oswald Mosley for £200,000.

On 29 March 1853 Manchester became a city, and in 1868 a new town hall was built on its present site, designed by Alfred Waterhouse. The old town hall was used as a reference library for some time, but was later demolished. In 1893 Manchester's chief magistrate was granted letters patent to become Lord Mayor.

The city boundaries changed several times over the years as more and more townships were absorbed into Manchester:

• 1838: Ardwick; Beswick; Cheetham; Chorlton-upon-Medlock; Hulme.
• 1885: Bradford; Moss Side (part); Rusholme; Withington (part); Harpurhey.
• 1890: Blackley; Clayton; Crumpsall; Gorton (part); Moston; Newton; Openshaw.
• 1901: Gorton (part).
• 1904: Burnage; Chorlton-cum-Hardy; Didsbury; Moss Side; Withington.
• 1909: Gorton (part); Levenshulme.
• 1931: Baguley; Etchells; Northenden.

There's a useful map of the changes from 1838–1931 on the Manchester UK website, www.manchester2002-uk.com/maps/manc 1938-map.html. See A. Redford, and I. Russell, *The History of Local Government in Manchester*, 3 vols (Longmans Green, 1939–40) and Shena D. Simon, *A Century of City Government 1838–1938* (Allen and Unwin, 1938).

After incorporation, the corporation made a real difference to its inhabitants' lives, for instance, by laying new sewers. The council bought out the Manchester and Salford Waterworks Company (which had previously acquired the manorial rights to the town's water). The Manchester Corporation Waterworks Company embarked on an ambitious scheme to bring fresh water to its thirsty citizens: it built reservoirs at Thirlmere in Derbyshire and at Woodhead in the Longdendale Valley. Demand for water continued to grow along with Manchester's population, and in the late 1920s the corporation began working on a new reservoir at Haweswater.

The council ended the building of new back-to-back houses in 1844, and reconditioned many old working class homes. Early in the twentieth century, a new housing estate was built at Blackley, and the new 'garden town' of Wythenshawe (comprising Baguley, Etchells and Northenden) was constructed after the area's amalgamation with Manchester in 1931.

The council controlled many aspects of its citizens' lives (and of course still does): traffic, industry and commerce, health and sanitation, street cleansing and refuse, gas (from 1843), electricity, education, social services, public parks, libraries, etc. See *How Manchester is Managed: A Record of Municipal Activity*, which was published annually between 1925 and 1939 (MCL has copies).

MCL(M) holds an extremely large collection of Manchester City Council archives, including 3,000 volumes of Manchester City Council minutes from 1810 to the 1980s. MCL holds the published proceedings of the Manchester Borough/City Council, 1838–2014; indexes are available for 1838–1962. The main MCC series are listed with approximate dates, and series reference numbers, in Table 4 opposite. This is not an exhaustive list, and readers should consult GMLives for further information. The MLIA website has an online guide to local government records, http://bit.ly/1Oxgbf6.

Some committee minutes are filed separately: Gaol Construction Committee, 1848–51 (M231/2/1/1–2); Manchester Gas Committee, 1824–1949 (M27); Tramways Committee, 1898–1964 (M29/1/4); Water Works Committee, 1848–1966 (M231); Health Committee, 1872–5 (M595/1/1–2).

MCL(M) also holds the Corporation Waterworks records, 1848–1966 (M231): minutes, order books, records of premises supplied, inspector's reports, changes of tenancy books, etc. This series includes records for the former Manchester and Salford Waterworks Company, 1814–41.

Table 4: Manchester City Council Records at MCL(M)

Department	Date	Ref.
Air Pollution Advisory Board	1912–14	M360
Architects and related department staff records	1889–2002	M771
Building Control Department records	1867–1986	M900
Cleansing Department	1805–1989	M595
Cleansing Department additional records	1836–1973	2008/37
Corporate Property records	1901–62	M899
Education Department schools' records	1850s–2002	M66
Education Department minutes incl. teachers	1900s–99	M428
Engineers' Archive (maps and plans)	1830s–1950s	M845
Engineers' and Surveyors' Department	1890–1969	M723
Finance Department	1890s–1960	M848
Hackney Coach Department	1925–52	M598
Health Department: canal boat records	1909–72	M487
Highways Department ledgers	1825–1973	M19
Housing Department compulsory purchase orders	1953–83	M646
Manchester Festival Office	1981–2001	M692
Market Inspector's court book	1890–1937	M736
Papers relating to mechanization of accounting and purchase of first mainframe computer	1931–99	M770
Parks and Cemeteries Department wages alteration books and wages advanced book	1915–57	M722
Personnel Department	1920s–90s	M844
Photographers' Department (street indexes available)	1939–2000s	M850
Town Clerk's Department papers: public functions	1857–1938	M68
Transport Department	1873–1969	M29
Watch Committee registers of licences	1889–1974	M192
Weights and Measures Department	1950–74	M417

The Building Control Department records are useful for exploring the area's architectural history, because the department kept plans of the city's buildings from late Victorian times until the 1980s. The series has been partially indexed on GMLives (limit your search by the reference number M900).

The Engineering and City Surveyor's Department (M723) created thousands of maps and plans for sewers, cemeteries, crematoria, schools, hospitals, power stations, housing estates, etc. This series is also partially indexed on GMLives. Health and education are discussed in Chapter 6.

SALFORD BEFORE AND AFTER INCORPORATION

As we saw earlier, Salford was governed by the Manchester and Salford Police Commissioners after 1792. In 1830 Salford's police commissioners separated from Manchester, and the Salford Improvement Act gave them extra powers to pave and widen streets and institute better lighting.

Like Manchester townships, individual Salford township records include Poor Law records, constables' accounts, apprenticeship indentures, etc. SCA holds several series of township records (see Table 5 below), some of which are on microfilm at SLHL. Handlists are available.

Table 5: Township Records at Salford City Archives

Township	Dates Covered	Series Ref.
Barton Moss	1894–1933	P6
Barton-upon-Irwell	1753–1963	P2
Broughton	1807–52	P3
Clifton	1825–1925	P4
Eccles (parish)	1899–1928	P5
Irlam	1895–1927	P7
Little Hulton	1732–1929	P6
Pendlebury	1839–1926	P8
Pendleton (parish)	1823–82	P9
Salford*	1662–1865	P10
Swinton	1895–1927	P11
Worsley	1687–1925	P12

* LA holds Salford township records, 1710–98 (PR2860), including settlement examinations and certificates, bastardy papers and apprenticeship records.

Salford was incorporated as a borough in 1844, and granted a coat of arms the same year. Part of Broughton township on the south side of the Irwell was included in the incorporation. Salford's first mayor was Sir William Lockett. The new Salford Borough Council replaced the role of the Salford Police Commissioners.

Then in 1853 Pendleton, the remaining part of Broughton, and part of Pendlebury merged with Salford; from this date the municipal borough boundaries co-existed with the parliamentary boundaries. In 1889 Salford became a county borough, but did not achieve city status until 1926.

The current administrative area of the City of Salford comprises the former local authorities which were part of the City (or County Borough) of Salford prior to the Local Government Act of 1972. In 1974 the former City became part of Salford Metropolitan District Council within GMC (see below), and this new Metropolitan District was given the title of City of Salford. Eccles Borough (formed 1892), Swinton and Pendlebury Borough (1894), Irlam Urban District and Worsley Urban District merged with Salford City Council.

Salford City Archives holds records of the Salford County Borough Council from 1672–1974 (L/CS/CL), including minutes, rate books, portmote records, coroner's records, etc. The series also includes the Salford Town Clerk collection, 1800–1980. Salford City Council records from 1974 onwards including minutes and maps are at SCA (S/); a handlist is available. Printed minutes of Salford City Council for 1973 onwards are in S/AMZ1.

SCA also holds records for Eccles Borough including minutes, rate books and maps, 1864–1974 (L/BE); Swinton and Pendlebury Urban District Council records, 1867–1974 (L/BSP); Irlam Urban District Council, 1895–1974 including rate books (L/DI), and Worsley Urban District Council records including rate books, 1879–1974 (L/DW). Handlists are available for these series.

Both Manchester and Salford had municipal gas supplies and the National Gas Archive at Warrington holds records, including administrative, financial, and staff, for Manchester Corporation gas works, 1824–1953 (NW: MAC) and Salford Corporation gas works, 1840–1964: (NW: SAC).

The relationship between Manchester and Salford has sometimes been less than cordial in the past. For example, Salford was dependent on Manchester for its water supply. But Salford alone was responsible for cleaning up the River Irwell, which was filled with pollution by towns higher upstream. Salford was also charged with attempting to deal with possible flooding, even though both cities were on the Irwell's banks. Over the years, proposals to merge Salford with its more populous neighbour have sparked great controversy, and this issue may not yet be moribund.

GREATER MANCHESTER COUNTY

The Local Government Act of 1972 reorganized local government throughout England and Wales. On 1 April 1974, Greater Manchester County (GMC) was formed, and Manchester and Salford became metropolitan districts within the new county. GMC contained ten metropolitan districts: Bolton, Bury, Oldham, Rochdale, Stockport, Tameside, Trafford, Wigan, Manchester and Salford. Manchester and Salford petitioned the Crown to keep their city and borough status, and both cities were granted a new charter that year.

For a detailed history of boundary changes for Manchester and Salford (with maps), see N.J. Frangopulo, *Tradition in Action: The Historical Evolution of the Greater Manchester County* (E.P. Publishing Ltd, 1977).

The whole GMC area was administered by the GMC Council from County Hall in Manchester; it controlled county wide functions such as the police and fire services. Each metropolitan district, including Manchester and Salford, had their own metropolitan district councils and looked after areas such as housing, education and libraries. MCL(G) holds records for the GMC Council, 1972–86 (this collection is mostly held off-site) (GMC).

Then in 1986, the GMC Council was abolished (although GMC still exists as a ceremonial county) and its metropolitan districts became new unitary authorities. Some functions of the GMC were transferred to the district councils. The county wide functions of the old GMC Council were taken over by a new body, the Association of Greater Manchester Authorities. Manchester City Council and Salford City Council each administer their own areas.

Archives for the other Metropolitan Borough Councils within the Greater Manchester area such as Tameside and Bolton are held in the record office for the appropriate district. For example, Tameside Local

Studies and Archive Centre hold Tameside Metropolitan Borough Council records, 1974–2012 (T). Explore GMLives and TNA Discovery for more information.

THE POOR
Poor Relief Before 1834

Until the 1940s, there was no national state provision for the poor, sick, destitute or mentally ill. Families relied on relatives for help, but when times were hard they turned to the parish or charity for aid. Under the Elizabethan Poor Laws, each parish took responsibility for its 'paupers'; aid was paid for by the 'poor rates'. Help ('poor relief') was given to people in poorhouses or workhouses; sometimes 'out-relief' such as food, blankets or money was given to people in their own homes.

People who were admitted to workhouses or poorhouses performed work in return for their keep such as picking oakum, breaking rocks for road-mending, spinning or weaving. The children of people in receipt of poor relief were usually apprenticed out to stop them being a 'burden' on the parish. After 1802 parishes kept registers of child apprentices; apprenticeship indentures may also survive (see Chapter 4). Parishes also paid for poor people's medical care and smallpox vaccinations.

Each parish or township only helped people who had a legal 'settlement' in their area. The parish authorities sought maintenance for illegitimate children from their putative fathers, and lying-in costs for destitute mothers. LA holds many examples of settlement 'examinations' (which often include family information), removal orders, bastardy bonds and child maintenance orders in its quarter sessions records. The QSP series includes petitions regarding the maintenance of persons sent to Salford Workhouse.

A workhouse for Manchester was proposed as early as 1731, but political wrangling in the town ensured that one was not built until 1754 in Cumberland Street. In 1763 it moved to Miller's Lane, but this building was later demolished. An Act of Parliament was passed in 1790 to enable Manchester to build a new poorhouse at New Bridge Street (Strangeways); this institution later had a fever hospital attached to it.

Salford's first workhouse was built in 1732; its first governor was John Rowe. It was replaced by a workhouse, built in 1793 at Greengate, which had room for 400 inmates. Two years later, the father of weaver poet Samuel Bamford became its master. However, by 1834 some townships still did not have their own workhouse; the Hulme, Chorlton-upon-Medlock and Ardwick authorities used those at Gorton and Blackley. See Gordon Bradley Hinde, *Provision for the Relief of the Poor in Manchester 1754–1826* (Chetham Society, 1975).

Some records are available for the earliest workhouses in the area at MCL(M). For example, a Poor House Book survives for the Strangeways workhouse, 1790–1811 (M3/3/5) and Blackley paupers' labour account books, 1824–41 (M10/4). The MLIA website has an online guide to its Poor Law records pre-1834, http://bit.ly/2iaFF8z.

JRL holds an early Manchester Churchwardens and Overseers' Account Book, 1664–1711 (English MS No. 97). CL's Booth Archive holds a notebook with a 'register of poor persons resident in Salford Workhouse 21 April 1732 with the time of their going out', which gives the name of the individual, their age and their reason for leaving the workhouse (Booth/2/9/1); a notebook with minutes discussing the appointment of a governor in 1732 (Booth/2/9/2); and a general Order Book, 1795–1806 with notes on meetings concerning Salford Workhouse (Booth/2/9/3).

Poor Relief After 1834

The cost of poor rates in Britain escalated as the population grew. The ruling elite suspected that the help people were given was a disincentive for them to work; they were more likely to breed fresh recipients for relief.

After the 1834 Poor Law Amendment Act, poor relief became the responsibility of groups of parishes called Unions, each administered by a Board of Guardians elected by ratepayers. They were supervised by the Poor Law Commission in London (later the Poor Law Board). However, the local churchwardens and overseers of the poor continued to be responsible for the collection of poor rates. TNA holds correspondence between the Poor Law Board and individual Unions, www.nationalarchives.gov.uk/help-with-your-research/research-guides/poverty-poor-laws/.

More workhouses were built, and a new, stricter regime introduced to make life in the workhouse as unpalatable as possible. Each workhouse had a master and matron. Inmates were forced to wear a uniform; the sexes were split, and families 'inside' were only permitted limited contact. It was thought that if children stayed with their parents, they would become 'pauperized' and reliant on relief.

One should not assume that a widow or orphan lived in the workhouse full-time. In March 1844, over 1,600 widows were in receipt of out-relief in Manchester, along with over 1,200 dependent children (*2nd Report . . . into the State of Large Towns*, Vol. I, 1844).

However, industrial towns like Manchester and Salford had little enthusiasm for the new Poor Law. Local parish overseers knew that if a factory closed, large numbers of people would need help at once; it was not always the case that workers were feckless and improvident. For the fight against the new Poor Law, see Nicholas C. Edsall, *The Anti-Poor Law Movement 1834–44* (Manchester University Press, 1971).

Gradually, parishes in northwest England were forced into line with the new law. Chorlton Union was the first in the Manchester area (1837), followed by Salford (1838); Manchester Union was formed in 1841. See Appendix 5 for a list of Poor Law Unions in Manchester and Salford with dates, and their constituent townships.

A workhouse for Chorlton Union was erected on Stretford New Road but was soon found to be too small. In 1854 a magnificent new workhouse was built at rural Withington, on Nell Lane; it had accommodation for over 1,500 persons. There's an online guide to its records held by MCL(M), which are available on microfilm, http://bit.ly/2i53HpC. LA holds Roman Catholic baptism and confirmation registers, and chaplains' report books, for Withington Workhouse and Hospital (RCWI Acc.9126).

The New Bridge Street Workhouse at Manchester was superseded by a brand new building (the Manchester Union Workhouse) at Crumpsall, on the 'Bongs' estate. New Bridge Street continued to care for the elderly and infirm until 1875. MLIA has an online guide to its records for New Bridge Street Workhouse and the Workhouse (later Hospital) at Crumpsall, http://bit.ly/2hVaKy0. See also Mark Greenwood, *Springfield Hospital: The Human History, 1855–1995* (Manchester Health Authority, 1997).

Another workhouse was built at Crumpsall for Prestwich Union in 1868 (this body previously had a workhouse at Rainsough). The records for Prestwich Union Workhouse have not survived, but some related material is in George Hill's papers at MCL(M) (M252).

Most workhouses became hospitals in the early twentieth century (see Chapter 6). After 1930, poor relief in Manchester was administered by MCC's Public Assistance Committee until 1948, when National Assistance was introduced.

Poor Law and Workhouse Records

Township records, parish vestry records, churchwarden and parish overseers' accounts, parish books and poorhouse or workhouse accounts are all rich sources (see Tables 3 and 5 earlier in this chapter for township records).

MCL(M) holds records of the Manchester churchwardens and overseers of the poor, 1651–1877 (M3). These are mostly administrative records; however, series M3/9 includes parish apprenticeship indentures. The Manchester Overseers' Library at MCL has many items relating to the Poor Law in the area. Records of the Manchester, Chorlton and Prestwich Unions, 1837–1948 are in series M4. MCL(M) also has details of staff employed in Manchester Union including Crumpsall Workhouse, New Bridge Street Workhouse and Swinton Schools; see the abstracts of accounts (339 M7) from the 1890s until 1930. Photos of local workhouses are itemized on GMLives and TNA Discovery. Unfortunately, the Manchester Board of Guardians' minute books were destroyed in the Manchester blitz.

SCA has minute books, 1838–1930 for Salford Union (L/GS) but the admission and discharge registers for Salford Workhouse were pulped during the Second World War. SCA's collection of Little Hulton township records (P6) include Overseers' Minute books, 1914–27. MLFHS members can access several documents relating to the Poor Law in Salford via the society's website.

LA holds the minutes for the Barton-upon-Irwell Union Board of Guardians, 1849–1930 and birth, death and creed registers, and medical officers' report books (PUE). Little Hulton, now in Salford, was in Bolton Poor Law Union from 1837, and surviving Poor Law records are held by Bolton Archives and Local Studies Services (GBO).

Workhouse, hospital and infirmary records usually include admission and discharge registers, staff records, vaccination registers and creed registers (1876 onwards). Creed registers give each inmate's name, date of birth, date and place of admission, creed, date of discharge or death; some include occupation, last address or details of next of kin. Vaccination registers were returns made to the vaccination officer of children's births and deaths. Findmypast's Manchester collection includes admission and discharge registers, and creed (religious) registers for several workhouses.

Peter Higginbotham's Workhouses website is probably the best free resource online, and the reader should take time to explore this comprehensive overview of the Poor Law system, www.work houses.org.uk/. It's packed with images and information, maps and plans. His Manchester and Salford pages include lists of workhouse staff and inmates in the 1881 census:

• www.workhouses.org.uk/Manchester/.
• www.workhouses.org.uk/Salford/.

Gerard Lodge's website also has a wealth of information on Manchester and Salford Poor Law records and workhouses, http:// bit.ly/1ZrNRkB, and Guardians' minutes, http://bit.ly/1r9WJj5.

Orphanages and Children's Homes
Many workhouse inmates were children; some of these institutions had schools attached. 'Industrial schools', sometimes known as 'barrack schools' or 'district schools', were large residential institutions for workhouse children. Manchester Union built the Swinton Industrial Schools (1846) which housed over 600 children. MLIA has an online guide to the records available, http://bit.ly/2gXrqmB.

After the mid-1870s, it became more common for pauper children to be 'boarded out' either with foster parents, or in 'cottage homes'. These homes were usually run by a married couple, and the children attended local schools. For example, early in the twentieth century, Salford Union built some cottage homes for children at Culcheth, and MCL(G) has a photographic collection (DPA/1679).

Chorlton Union's cottage homes were built at Styal, in rural Cheshire. MCL(M) holds Styal Cottage Homes admission registers and registers of children , 1903–62 (M66/84 – restricted access). This series includes lists of children who were sent to Canada as migrants. In mid-to-late Victorian times, philanthropists, children's homes, charities (including Barnardo's) and workhouses began sending children to places like Australia and Canada to begin new lives as farm or domestic servants. These children often endured great hardships in their new homes.

Poor Law union records include 'registers of boarded out children' or 'registers of orphan children' which give the child's name, age, the address of the foster parent or cottage home, and dates when the child was living there. Sometimes information is given on the child's later whereabouts, e.g. if they returned to the workhouse or went into domestic service. The Salford Poor Law Union records at SCA include minutes for the Boarding-Out Committee.

In 1870, Sunday school teachers Leonard Kilbee Shaw, Annie Shaw and Richard Bramwell Taylor founded a charity for destitute children, the Manchester and Salford Boys' and Girls' Refuges and Homes. It set up several homes for boys and girls in places like Broughton and Angel Meadow. The charity also sent child migrants to Canada. Over the years, the charity greatly expanded its activities, and is still helping children and families. MCL(M) holds records for Manchester and Salford Boys' and Girls' Refuges and Homes from 1870–1930 (M189 – restricted access). The charity, now known as the Together Trust, has an archive relating to children who were in its care. The website has a list of children's homes run by the charity: https://www.togethertrust.org.uk/our-history. Contact the archivist for family history enquiries, https://www.togethertrust.org.uk/contact-us. There's an archive blog: http://togethertrustarchive.blogspot.co.uk/.

The Former Children's Homes website, www.childrenscottage homes.org.uk, and Peter Higginbotham's Children's Homes websites have lots more information, www.childrenshomes.org.uk.

CHARITIES AND FRIENDLY SOCIETIES
People in need could also obtain recommendations ('tickets') for help such as food, clothing and blankets from local charities; poor children were also bound as apprentices. The Borough-Reeve's Charity (later the Mayor's Charity) was funded by benefactions such as the Clarke and Marshall charities, funded by rents and profits from these charities' lands. MCL(M)'s collections of the records of Clarke's and Marshall's Charities, 1653–1909 include accounts, rentals and maps (M5). Parish churchwardens and overseers also distributed aid funded by benefactions such as Mayer's and Sutton's charities.

During the early nineteenth century and later, the Charity Commissioners investigated charities throughout Britain to check that their funds were properly used. See, for example, the *16th Report of the*

Charity Commissioners, County Palatine of Lancaster Reports: Manchester (1826). In 1853 a statutory body was set up to oversee charities. MCL(G) holds the Charity Commissioners' accounts for the Manchester and Salford area, 1846–1959 (A6).

Humphrey Booth the Elder (1580–1635) and his grandson Humphrey Booth the Younger left lands for the relief of the poor and the upkeep of Trinity Church, Salford. These long-established charities also funded medical care and housing for the elderly. CL holds the archive of the Humphrey Booth Charities; there's an online guide, http://chethams.org.uk/wp-content/uploads/sites/3/2016/09/chethams_library_booth_charities_collection.pdf.

John Caldwell's charity is another long-established foundation in Salford; the money was used to buy food and fuel for the poor. SCA holds an account book, 1759–1960 (U40).

One way in which workers helped each other was by the formation of friendly societies such as sickness and burial clubs. Friendly societies, savings banks and clubs such as scientific societies had to register their rules with JPs at quarter sessions. LA holds enrolment, registration and deposit records, 1794–1897 (QDS). Several friendly societies are listed on GMLives; for example, MCL(G) holds records for the National Independent Order of the Oddfellows Friendly Society, 1875–2001 (ODD).

Many other charities sprang up in Manchester and Salford. As will be shown in the next chapter, some charitable foundations concentrated on education and were responsible for some of the region's most famous schools.

THE TEMPERANCE MOVEMENT

The temperance movement grew up during the nineteenth century to combat the many social problems caused by drink. The Independent Order of Rechabites, a friendly society, was founded in Salford in 1835. The Manchester and Salford Temperance Society was formed in Oak Street the same year; Joseph Brotherton was president of its Salford branch. The movement gained thousands of members and spread out overseas.

Temperance societies, leagues, guilds, Independent Order of Rechabite tents and Band of Hope records such as account books, minute books, pledge books, abstainers' registers, certificates, photographs, etc. may be archived with parish or chapel collections such as Sunday school records. The Manchester Women's Christian Temperance Association (1875) had a mission at the Police Court. MCL(M) holds records for the association, 1880–2000 including attendance registers (M286).

The Senate House Library, University of London holds records for the Independent Order of Rechabites, www.senatehouselibrary. ac.uk/our-collections/special-collections. The University of Central Lancashire holds the Joseph Livesey temperance collections; some images of the collection are online, https://www.uclan.ac.uk/students/ study/library/livesey_collection .php.

Further Reading

Bateman, John, *History and Description of the Manchester Waterworks*, Manchester, 1884

Fowler, Simon, *Poor Law Records for Family Historians*, Family History Partnership, 2011

Garrard, John, *Leadership and Power in Victorian Industrial Towns 1830–80*, Manchester University Press, 1983

Gibson, Jeremy and Youngs, Frederic A., *Poor Law Union Records: 4. Gazetteer of England and Wales*, 2nd edn, FFHS, 1997

Harwood, J.J., *History and Description of the Thirlmere Water Scheme*, Manchester, 1895

Midwinter, E.C., *Social Administration in Lancashire 1830–1860*, Manchester University Press, 1969

Sumner, Jeremy and Rogers, Colin, *Poor Law Union Records 2: Midlands and Northern England*, 3rd edn, Family History Partnership, 2008

Webb, Beatrice and Webb, Sidney, *English Local Government: English Poor Law History*, 2 vols, Longmans, 1927

Webb, Sidney and Beatrice, *English Local Government: Statutory Bodies for Special Purposes*, 2 vols, Longmans, Green & Co., 1922

Chapter 6

HEALTH AND EDUCATION

INFIRMARIES, DISPENSARIES, ASYLUMS AND HOSPITALS

Poor people who could not afford to pay for the services of a surgeon, physician or apothecary relied on charities and voluntary bodies. Manchester Infirmary was founded in 1752 at Shudehill by Joseph Bancroft and local surgeon Charles White; Joseph Massey provided funding for the new institution. By the end of its first year the infirmary had treated 75 patients and 249 out-patients. Four years later the infirmary moved to Piccadilly (on the site of the present Piccadilly Gardens). A House of Recovery, or fever hospital, opened near the infirmary in 1796.

The infirmary was an important training institution for local doctors. By the early twentieth century, the old building was no longer suitable and a new Royal Infirmary opened on Oxford Road in 1909. See W. Brockbank, *Portrait of a Hospital 1752–1948* (W. Heinemann, 1952).

Access for poor people to an institution like the infirmary was by recommendation. The institution's subscribers or patrons were allotted a set number of recommendations per year; a poorly person had to obtain a written note from a subscriber before they could obtain treatment. However, the infirmary accepted accident cases without a note.

In 1790 a Lying-In Charity for poor married women was set up on Salford Bridge. Most women gave birth at home, but concerned local citizens felt that mothers who were destitute should have somewhere safe and clean to have their babies. The charity also trained midwives. Five years later, the charity moved to Stanley Street in Salford, but the new premises proved too expensive and after 1811 it focused on providing care to women in their own homes. The charity was later re-named St Mary's Hospital and Dispensary; by 1890 it had moved to Oxford Road.

Several specialist institutions grew up in the Manchester area. An eye institution was founded on Faulkner Street in 1815; it later moved to St John's Street. Lock House (1819) in Bond Street was dedicated to the treatment of venereal disease.

The poor could also get access to medical care at charitable dispensaries; the resident physicians attended patients in their own homes. The Infirmary had a dispensary attached to it. There was also the Ardwick and Ancoats Dispensary on Great Ancoats Street, the Chorlton Row Dispensary and the Salford and Pendleton Dispensary on Broken Bank.

Some workhouses, but not all, had a sick ward or infirmary. Poor Law Unions eventually responded to the need to keep patients separate from other inmates, especially if suffering from infectious diseases like typhus and tuberculosis. Booth Hall Hospital was built early in the twentieth century for Prestwich Union. It was used as a military hospital during the early part of the First World War, but in 1915 it became a children's hospital – one of the largest in the UK (MCL(M), M302). See Raymond Hargreaves, *The Story of Booth Hall Hospital: curing and caring for northern children* (Ross Anderson, 1987).

Several specialist institutions were in the care of the Manchester Board of Guardians shortly before its dissolution, including Langho and some children's homes, http://bit.ly/2iaR6wZ. Langho was a hospital for epileptics built by Chorlton and Manchester Asylum Committee (MCL(M), M464). The board also maintained a fleet of ambulances.

Henshaw's Blind Asylum was founded at Manchester in 1835 following a legacy by Thomas Henshaw, an Oldham hat manufacturer. JRL has records of Henshaw's Society For Blind People (formerly the Asylum) for 1833–1982 which include minutes and financial accounts, correspondence, etc. (HEN). Trafford Local Studies holds records for the society including correspondence, annual reports, photographs, deeds, documents and the will and codicil of Thomas Henshaw (TRA1727).

For a detailed overview of the growth of hospitals in Manchester, Salford and the surrounding areas, with copious references, see John V. Pickstone, *Medicine and Industrial Society: A History of Hospital Development in Manchester and Its Region 1752–1946* (Manchester University Press, 1985).

In the eighteenth century, it was unusual for provincial towns to have an institution that catered for mentally ill people or 'lunatics'. They were often placed in the workhouse or poorhouse, without any segregation from the other inmates. The Lunatic Hospital and Asylum was added to Manchester Infirmary in 1766; it opened the following year. Conditions in these early asylums were often extremely poor; inmates were given straw bedding and were chained up for hours.

Thanks to the work of reformers like Lord Shaftesbury, society gradually realized that mentally ill people needed more humane treatment. When Prestwich Asylum opened in 1851 it was one of the largest in Europe, and treated thousands of patients from Manchester and Salford. LA has minutes, patients and admission registers, staff registers, reception orders, 1847–1978 (QAM/6). MCL(G) holds staff and patient records, 1851–1973 (A/PRES). There's an index to admissions on Findmypast. The asylum was later re-named Prestwich Hospital, and MCL(G) holds nursing records from the 1920s (Access. 1814) and twentieth-century patient records on microfiche (A/PRES add). Workhouse and Poor Law records, and hospital records are also discussed in Chapter 5.

MLFHS members can access several useful hospital and workhouse databases via the society's website. There's an index to patient admissions for Whittingham Hospital (Asylum) admissions register, 1851–1901 for patients from Manchester and Salford between 1873 and 1913. There's also an index to patient admissions to Prestwich Asylum, 1851–1901 for the first fifty years from its opening. An index for the Salford Workhouse Visiting Committee Minutes, 1865–1915 has over 26,000 names. A Lancashire Workhouse Inmates, 1861 database has names of 1,200 inmates who had been residents for more than 5 years. Another list gives the addresses of Lancashire and Cheshire workhouses. From 1904 onwards, where a child was born in a workhouse, only the address of the workhouse was entered on the birth certificate, not the institution's name.

Wellcome Library Hospital Records Database
This free searchable database includes over twenty Manchester and Salford institutions such as Grangethorpe, the Manchester Victoria Memorial Jewish Hospital, Royal Manchester Children's Hospital and Salford Royal. Search by hospital name or by town. When you find the hospital you want, click on the link to find details of the dates it was in use, administrative authorities (e.g. county council), types of surviving

records held and their location, as well as any relevant finding aids, www.nationalarchives.gov.uk/hospitalrecords/search.asp.

If researching the history of a hospital, you may also find the Voluntary Hospitals Database useful, www.hospitalsdatabase.lshtm. ac.uk/. 'Zoom' in on the map to find hospitals in a particular area. You can download data or spreadsheets for information such as hospital income, number of beds, staffing levels, etc.

MANCHESTER BOARD OF HEALTH

In the late eighteenth century, Dr Thomas Percival and other local medical men became greatly concerned by the prevalence of fever in the manufacturing districts. They formed the Manchester Board of Health in 1796 to look into the causes and prevention of fever.

Working class houses had no piped running water and no modern sanitation. Only upper class homes had water closets. Poor families used a privy midden (a wooden seat on top of a hole in the ground lined with brick), or the 'pail and pan' method, or a common privy in the street. The contents of cesspools and privy middens often contaminated water supplies. Families without a privy threw the contents of their chamber-pots into the street or stored it on dung-heaps outside.

During the cholera epidemic of the early 1830s the Manchester Board of Health inspected 6,951 houses and discovered that 2,221 (about one-third) had no privy at all. A decade later, in the neighbourhood of Oldham Road and St George's Road, had 'only 33 petties [privies] for 7,095 persons, or 1 to 215 inhabitants' and hence were 'in the most disgusting state of filth' (*2nd Report . . . into the State of Large Towns*, Vol. I, 1844). Many people lived in jerry-built 'back-to-backs'.

There were also 18,200 people living in 4,400 cellar dwellings in Manchester. In 1,500 cellars, 3 people shared the same bed, and there were even a couple of instances of 8 people sharing a bed. In Salford, 41 working class dwellings were visited by the board; there were 281 people living in them, but only 54 bedrooms, so on average about 5 people shared each bedroom.

Manchester-born sanitary reformer Edwin Chadwick conducted a major investigation into Britain's living conditions in 1842. The infectious diseases that circulated during this period were no respecters of persons – the gentry were just as vulnerable to diseases like cholera and typhus. Chadwick discovered that in Manchester, the average age of death of 'professional persons and gentry' was 38 years; that of 'mechanics, labourers and their families' was just 17 years. Over half the children born in Manchester died before they were 5 years old.

MCL(M) holds minutes/proceedings of the Manchester Board of Health, 1831–3 (M9/36), and papers relating to the foundation and early years of the Board of Health, 1796–1804 (available on microfilm).

MLFHS has compiled a list of 200 Manchester cholera victims noted in a report by Henry Gaulter, *The Origin and Progress of the Malignant Cholera in Manchester* (1833). Gaulter included the name, age and brief address for each victim, as well as highly detailed lifestyle or environmental conditions which may have made them more susceptible to the disease. The database is available to the society's members online, and is also in Findmypast's Manchester Collection.

Manchester City Council appointed its first Medical Officer of Health (MOH) in 1867. MOH reports were published annually, and local reference libraries may have copies.

The recurrence of epidemics, and high mortality rates, led Manchester doctors to expand their knowledge and keep abreast of the latest developments in medicine. The Manchester Medical Society was founded in 1839; a history of the society and its library is online, www.mms.org.uk/our-history.

The Manchester Medical Collection of books (MMC at the University of Manchester Archives and Records Centre (UoMARC)), founded by Ernest Bosdin Leech, forms part of the University's Medical Archives collections, bit.ly/1RzGkuv. The collections include the archives of several local medical associations such as the Society of Medical Officers of Health, North-Western Branch, 1875–1981 (NWH), and the Association of Certifying Factory Surgeons, 1892–1969 (CFS). The personal papers of several Manchester doctors form part of the collections, which can be accessed by appointment in the main University of Manchester Library.

For a brief history of the Manchester Medical Society, and biographical sources for local doctors (including Salford), see W.J. Elwood and A.F. Tuxford, *Some Manchester Doctors: A Biographical Collection* (Manchester University Press, 1984).

SCHOOLS AND EDUCATION
Early Grammar Schools

The earliest educational foundation in Manchester may be one founded by Richard Beswick. In 1506 Beswick endowed the Jesus Chapel of the Collegiate Church, and one of the priests attached to this chantry was required to keep a free school.

Then in 1515 Hugh Oldham, Bishop of Exeter, decided to found a free grammar school at Manchester for poor boys or scholars. Oldham's birthplace is not known for certain, but it seems likely that he was Manchester-born, perhaps from Crumpsall. Among the endowments given to the new school were the profits of the lord of the manor's three mills on the River Irk. Children from any county were permitted to study at Manchester Free Grammar School. See J.A. Graham and B.A. Phythian, *The Manchester Grammar School 1515–1965* (Manchester University Press, 1965).

One of the grammar school's most famous scholars was Hugh Chetham (1580–1653), a prosperous textile merchant. In his will dated 1651 he left £7,000 to buy an estate to fund the education of forty poor boys from the age of 6 to 14 years, after which they were to be bound as apprentices. Boys from Manchester, Salford, Crumpsall, Bolton, Droylesden and Turton townships were admitted. Chetham also left £1,000 for the foundation of a free library. The Chetham scholars were dressed in blue and yellow, with a blue cap and stockings.

The derelict building of the old college (of the Collegiate Church) was used for the new college (later known as Chetham's Hospital); it was close to the grammar school. The hospital became Chetham's School of Music in 1969. See A. Nicholson, *The Chetham Hospital and Library* (Sherratt & Hughes, 1901).

The records, including admission registers, and photos, for Manchester Free Grammar School are now held at the school's own archive, https://www.mgsarchives.org/. CL holds records of pupils who studied at Chetham's Hospital from 1635–1935.

Elementary Education

At the beginning of the nineteenth century, the children of well-off families were educated at home or in private schools. There was no state education for working class children. Social unrest gave rise to worries about illiteracy; if ordinary people could read their Bible, perhaps they would learn to accept their place in society.

As many children helped their families by going to work, Sunday schools were a good way to help them learn to read. In 1782, John Lancaster and Mr Fildes opened a Sunday school in a Manchester cellar. Two years later, Mr S. Newton funded a Sunday school building in Gun Street, Ancoats.

By the 1830s over 4,600 Manchester children attended Sunday schools, but only about 250 attended day schools. Manchester Collegiate Church had a Sunday school and a day school (1835) in Todd Street, Long Millgate. St John's Church also had a day school, which was endowed in the early 1770s; young girls were given moral and religious training, and learned needlework. Salford had over thirty Sunday schools.

James Wheeler, *Manchester: Its Political, Social and Commercial History* (Manchester, 1836), provides a list of Sunday schools in existence in the early 1930s. CL holds the records (1784–1939) for the Manchester Sunday School, including minute books and subscription records (MUN.A.4.65–66 and MUN.A.6.3–6).

Daytime schooling was gradually introduced using the 'monitorial' method in 'Lancasterian' and 'National' schools. 'Lancasterian' (after founder Joseph Lancaster), or 'British' schools, were run by Dissenters under the auspices of the British and Foreign School Society.

'National' schools were Anglican schools, and these schools received the lion's share of government funding after some state aid was granted in 1833. Other denominations such as Roman Catholics, Jews and Quakers set up their own schools.

Some children were so destitute that they could not even attend Sunday schools and 'ragged' schools grew up to meet these children's needs. MCL(M) holds records for the Manchester and Salford Ragged School Union, 1858–1972.

In 1834 the Manchester Statistical Society surveyed the state of elementary education in Manchester and found that its quality was extremely poor. Around 43,300 children attended school; about 21 per cent of the population (school attendance was not compulsory at this date). Each child paid a few pence per week for their education. Little progress was made for many years because charities and voluntary societies could not cope with the large numbers of children who needed education.

Charter Street Ragged School, Angel Meadow (formerly Angel Meadow Ragged School). (© Sue Wilkes)

A number of societies were formed locally to promote educational reform, including the Lancashire Public School Association, formed in 1847 in Manchester. Its members included Jacob Bright (brother of the famous politician) and Richard Cobden. (At this date 'public' schools meant publicly funded schools, not the misnamed public schools of today which are really private schools.)

The association (later the National Public School Association) wanted free, secular, universal education for all children funded by local rates. It was opposed by the Manchester and Salford Committee on Education, which also wanted more school places, but under the control of religious bodies. Dr James Kay-Shuttleworth, a Manchester health and educational reformer, strongly supported the latter committee's work. MCL(M) holds the National Public School Association's minutes, papers and correspondence, 1840–62 (M136).

At last, Forster's Education Act of 1870 set up 'School Boards' with powers to build schools in areas where there were no church or voluntary schools. Manchester School Board was the first to be founded in the UK. Two prominent members of the new Board were Herbert Birley and Lydia E. Becker, an important local campaigner for women's suffrage. The first new school built by the board was in Vine Street, Hulme (1875). Manchester School Board records, including minutes, 1870–1904 are held at MCL(M) (M65). SCA holds Salford School Board minutes, 1870–1903 (L/SBS).

After the Taunton Commission (1868) found that most educational endowments had been appropriated by boys' schools, interest grew in providing secondary education for girls. Manchester High School for Girls, an independent school, was founded in 1873 at Portland Place in Oxford Road. The school has its own archive, www.mhsgarchive.org. See S.A. Burstall, *The Story of Manchester High School for Girls 1871–1911* (Manchester University Press, 1911).

Following the 1902 Education Act, school boards disappeared and were replaced by local education authorities (LEAs) controlled by county councils. The new LEAs had powers to set up secondary schools (county or municipal).

Salford Grammar School started out as Salford Municipal Secondary School for Boys (1904); the school was located at various sites before a purpose-built building was erected on Eccles Old Road, which opened in 1956. When comprehensive education was introduced in 1973, the grammar school merged with Pendleton High School for Girls to form Buile Hill High School.

School Records and Archives

MCL(M)'s main series of school records (M66) for MCC closed schools, and church schools, include admission registers, staff registers, log books and accident books. Pre-1925 school admission registers are available on microfilm; surviving admission registers have been digitized and are part of the Findmypast Manchester collection.

There's an online guide to local educational administration, and Manchester school records, http://bit.ly/1ZBrj0X. This guide includes series references for board schools which are not online, and some ragged schools and high schools. MCL(M) also holds MCC Education Committee records, including photos of officers and councillors, *c.*1890–1999 (M822).

SCA holds records for several schools and Sunday schools in the area. The Bridgewater Estates Archive (BEA) at UoS also contains materials relating to Salford schools, including photos. LA holds records for Roman Catholic schools in the Diocese of Salford (RCSF 4).

See S.E. Maltby, *Manchester and the Movement for National Elementary Education 1800–1870* (Manchester University Press, 1918). See also C.B. Bolton, 'The Development of Public Education in Manchester 1800–1902' and W.T. Stevenson, 'Features of the Expansion of Education under the Local Authority', in N. Frangopulo (ed.), *Rich Inheritance: A Guide to the History of Manchester* (Manchester Education Committee, 1963). This work includes a chronological list of Manchester Board Schools.

Industrial Schools and Reformatories

Industrial schools grew out of the ragged school movement. Charities and voluntary groups set up industrial schools for destitute children, especially children with previous criminal convictions (workhouses were reluctant to look after these children). These schools should not be confused with workhouse industrial schools run by Poor Law authorities. Both types of industrial school trained children so that they could earn their own living. The Manchester and Salford Reformatory for Juvenile Criminals started out as a ragged school. The reformatory moved to Poulton-le-Fylde in 1905.

LA holds reports, accounts and pupil records, 1853–1973 (DDX 1791). Some newspaper cuttings on the reformatory are at MCL(G): the Mary Turner collection, Box 18. MCL(M) holds records for Manchester Certified Industrial Schools (M369) including a minute book. Findmypast's Manchester collection includes Manchester Certified Industrial School, Ardwick Green, 1866–1912; Barnes Home, Heaton Mersey, 1867–1908; and Manchester Certified Industrial Schools, Branch for Girls, Sale, 1883–1904.

Gerald Lodge's website has information on Manchester Certified Industrial Schools, www.manchester-family-history-research.co.uk/new_page_2.htm.

Secondary Education and Universities

Secondary education in the Manchester area grew out of the Mechanics' Institutes movement. Manchester Mechanics' Institution (Institute), thought to be the first in England, was founded in 1824 on Cooper Street; a member's subscription cost 5s. per quarter. Engineer William Fairbairn, manufacturer Richard Roberts and Thomas Hopkins (members of Manchester's famous Literary and Philosophical Society) provided funds. Scientific lectures were given and members had access to a library. The institution later moved to David Street. See Mabel Tycote, *The Mechanics' Institutes of Lancashire and Yorkshire before 1851* (Manchester University Press, 1957).

Owens College was endowed by John Owens (1790–1846), a Manchester merchant. Its first home was Richard Cobden's former residence on Quay Street. The university was non-sectarian, and was considered particularly strong in science subjects. At first, college students in northwest England could not take a degree at their 'home' educational institution; they had to take external examinations from bodies such as the University of London.

When the Victoria University, Manchester (a federation of Owens College with Leeds and Liverpool colleges) was founded in 1880, it was authorized to offer degrees to students. See Joseph Thompson, *The Owens College: Its Foundation and Growth* (J.E. Cornish, 1886); H.B. Charlton, *Portrait of a University* (Manchester University Press, 1951); and Edward Fiddes, *Chapters in the History of Owens College and Manchester University 1851–1914* (Manchester University Press, 1937).

The university's administrative history is complex and some record

Owens College, Oxford Road, Manchester (later the University of Manchester).
Our Own Country (*Cassell & Co., c.1883), Vol. III. (Author's collection)*

series include collections from predecessor bodies. The University of Manchester Archives (MS) at UoMARC include the archives of several educational institutions. Owens College records cover 1828–1909 (OCA); the federal Victoria University collections, including minutes, cover 1880–1903 (FVU); and the University of Manchester Council Archive, 1880–2004 (UCO). There's an online guide, www.library. manchester.ac.uk/search-resources/guide-to-special-collections/uom archives/guide.

As the nineteenth century advanced, there were fears that Britain was lagging behind other industrial nations because of a shortage of technical instruction. Manchester and Salford were working towns, and it was difficult for people to further their education unless they could take classes in the evenings. In 1892 Manchester Corporation founded the Manchester Municipal Technical School, which eventually grew into the University of Manchester Institute of Science and Technology

(UMIST). The UMIST archives, 1892–2004 (TGB) at UoMARC include its predecessors the Manchester Mechanics' Institution minute books, annual reports and publications, 1824–1891 (MMI); the Manchester Municipal School of Technology, and the Manchester College of Science and Technology.

Student union collections at UoMARC include the University of Manchester Students Union archive from 1851 to the present (SUA) and the UMIST Students Union archive 1910–2004 (TSU). More information regarding the archival collections is available on the UoM online catalogue ELGAR, http://archives.li.man.ac.uk/ead.

In the Salford area, the Pendleton Mechanics' Institution (Institute) was founded in 1850, and the Salford Working Men's College was

The School of Art on Cavendish Street, Manchester. Illustration by H.E. Tidmarsh, Manchester Old and New *(Cassell & Co., c.1894), Vol. II. (Author's collection)*

formed eight years later. These two bodies later merged to form the Salford Royal Technical Institute, a forerunner of the University of Salford.

The University of Salford also has a complex administrative history, www.salford.ac.uk/about-us/heritage. The University of Salford Archives and Special Collections include records for Salford Grammar School, 1903–89 comprising report books, admission registers, staff registers, photos, etc. (SGS); Salford Royal Technical Institute and Royal Technical College records, 1896–1959 (RTI); and the Salford Technical and Engineering Association, *c*.1897–1977 (STE).

Women faced an uphill struggle to gain access to a university education. Although they attended lectures at the Manchester Mechanics' Institution, and later lectures, at Owens College, they were not permitted to study full-time and take examinations. (John Owens' will prohibited women students.) In 1877 the Manchester and Salford College for Women was founded to give higher instruction to young ladies in subjects like the arts and classics (UoMARC (MCW)).

Changes in the law in the 1870s made it possible for women to study at Owens College, but it was not until almost the end of the century that women students achieved parity with male students. For example, suffragette Christabel Pankhurst, who had attended Manchester High School for Girls, was a law graduate of the University of Manchester – but was not allowed to practise as a barrister. See Mabel Tylcote, *The Education of Women at Manchester University 1883 to 1933* (Manchester University Press, 1951). For more information on school and university records and researching educational history, see Sue Wilkes, *Tracing Your Ancestors' Childhood* (Pen & Sword, 2013).

SPORT AND FOOTBALL

Sports club news, including school sports, was often reported in local newspapers, with photos, especially if a team won a trophy. Local archives may have sports photos in their collections.

To find the records for a sporting club or association, search TNA Discovery catalogue, then click on 'Record Creators'. For example, a quick search using the terms 'Manchester' and 'football' elicits several results, such as the Manchester Schools Football Association. Its records (1895–2014), which include minutes, handbooks and photographs, are held at MCL(M): M829.

Manchester United Football Club originated in a railwaymen's football club at Newton Heath, formed in 1878, www.manutd.com/en/Club/History-By-Decade.aspx. The Manchester United Museum holds the archive collections, 1890–2006 (MSS) for its eponymous club including minute books, annual reports, magazines and scrapbooks: www.manutd.com/en/Visit-Old-Trafford/Museum-And-Stadium-Tour/Museum.aspx. You can download a scanned list of its holdings, http:// bit.ly/1sL4mxn.

Manchester City Football Club began life as St Mark's Club at Gorton in 1880. The club also has a museum at its stadium; the club's archive includes historical materials and photos, https://mancity.com/en/fans-and-community/club/club-history. Manchester is also home to the National Football Museum, which opened in 2012 in the Urbis building.

LIBRARIES

Apart from CL (which was not a lending library), there were no free libraries for the general public. Institutions like the classically elegant Portico Library on Mosley Street (1806), founded by the Manchester

In Peel Park, Salford. Our Own Country (Cassell & Co., n.d., c.1883), Vol. III. (Author's collection)

Portico Library, Manchester. (© Sue Wilkes)

Literary and Philosophical Society, were subscription-only (£2 10s. a year in the 1830s). Salford had a subscription library as early as 1771; it later moved to Manchester, and by 1834 the library was on Market Street. A subscription cost 16s. annually, and a library ticket cost a whopping 3 guineas in 1834. (For comparison, a hand-loom weaver's weekly wage was 5s. 6d.)

The foundation of municipal libraries also played a vital role in education for the working classes. Thanks to the efforts of Salford MP Joseph Brotherton, Mayor E.R. Langworthy and others, Britain's first free municipal library was founded in Peel Park, Salford in 1849. The Salford Royal Free Museum and Library (now Salford Museum and Art Gallery) opened in January the following year.

Manchester's Free Library opened in 1852 at Campfield. The library collections grew and grew, and the institution had several homes before Central Library, a magnificent building designed by E. Vincent Harris, opened in St Peter's Square in 1934. See B. Mullen, *The Royal Museum and Libraries* (Salford, 1899) and David Chadwick, *Free Public Libraries and Museums* (London, 1857).

FURTHER READING

Chadwick, Edwin, *Inquiry into The Sanitary Condition of the Labouring Population of Great Britain*, London, 1842

Cook, John, *Swinton Industrial School: Manchester Union, Moral, and Industrial Training School*, Swinton and Pendlebury Local History Society, 2007

Guest, Albert E., *Swinton Industrial Schools: an historical sketch and personal reminiscences*, Swinton and Pendlebury Public Libraries, 1961

Higginbotham, Peter, *The Workhouse Encyclopedia*, History Press, 2014

Higgs, Michelle, *Tracing Your Medical Ancestors*, Pen & Sword, 2011

James, Gary, *Manchester: A Football History*, James Ward, 2008

Mumford, Alfred A., *Manchester Grammar School 1515–1915*, Longmans, Green & Co., 1919

O'Brien, E., *Pauper in the Palace: Life in Swinton Industrial Schools*, Neil Richardson, 1977

Pratt, T., *The Portico Library, Manchester: Its History and Associations 1802–1922*, Sherratt & Hughes, 1922

Roberts, Jacqueline, *Working Class Housing in Nineteenth Century Manchester: the example of John St, Irk Town 1826–1936*, N. Richardson, n.d.

Chapter 7

COURT RECORDS, ESTATES, CRIME AND TAXATION

SALFORD HUNDRED

The early story of the Manchester district is lost in the mists of time. It is known that the Romans had a fort in the Castlefield area of the modern city; then darkness descends until the early tenth century. The Anglo-Saxon Chronicle records that King Edward the Elder (son of Alfred the Great) ordered the old Roman fort to be reinforced and manned as a defence against Norse invaders.

At this date England was divided into 'hundreds' or 'wapentakes', and each hundred was further subdivided into manors and townships, or vills. There were six hundreds situated between the Rivers Ribble and Mersey: Blackburn, Leyland, Newton, Salford, Warrington and West Derby. Manchester was little more than a hamlet in Salford Hundred.

Salford was a royal manor. The Domesday Book (1086) affirms that 'King Edward held Salford' before the Norman Conquest. Afterwards William the Conqueror gave the lands between the Ribble and the Mersey to his relative Roger of Poitou. Roger rewarded his own followers with grants of land; his knight Nigel was given a 'fief' of lands, and this area presently became the barony of Manchester. However, Salford manor was not part of this new barony: Roger of Poitou kept it for his own use (a 'demesne' manor).

Now Roger held lands in several parts of Britain, and because he had a castle at Lancaster, his estates became known as the 'honour of Lancaster'. This was the forerunner of the Duchy of Lancaster. Roger forfeited his lands in south Lancashire after rebelling against the king, but they were later returned to him in 1087 by William Rufus.

Around this time, Albert de Grelley (or Greslet) became owner of the barony of Manchester and the estate stayed with the Grelley family until the early 1300s. The barony of Manchester included lands in Salford, Leyland and West Derby hundreds. Part of Manchester barony was a 'desmene' manor. For a map of Manchester manor in 1300, see G.H. Tupling, 'Medieval and Early Modern Manchester', in *Manchester and Its Region: A Survey* (Manchester University Press, 1962).

Roger of Poitou rebelled again and forfeited his lands once more. After several changes of ownership, Salford manor became owned permanently by the Crown in Henry IV's reign, and our present Sovereign is lord of the manor of Salford.

The manors, in their turn, were divided into lesser manors (berewicks). The 'Medieval Documentation for Salford Hundred' website has information on archival sources and published records, https://salfordhundred.wordpress.com/. However, for ecclesiastical purposes, Salford Hundred was divided into eleven parishes, including Ashton, Eccles, Flixton, Manchester and Middleton. There's an index map for Salford Hundred on British History Online, www.british-history.ac.uk/vch/lancs/vol4/pp171-173.

Because the manors of Manchester and Salford had different owners, they each had their own administration. The lord of the manor held a regular court ('court baron') where tenancy disputes were sorted out and the lord asserted his privileges. Manorial tenants included 'freeholders' with no time limit to their tenure, and 'copyholders'. Their tenancies were recorded on the court rolls. Copyholders paid an 'entry fine' to the manor when they became tenants, in addition to paying rent, and this fine was recorded as an 'admittance'. Copyhold could be inherited, and the names of family members are often mentioned in the rolls. See P.B. Park, *My Ancestors Were Manorial Tenants* (Society of Genealogists, 2002).

In 1227, Robert de Grelley asked Henry III for the right to hold an annual fair in Manchester. It was held at Acres Field, now the site of St Ann's Square. Salford's first market and fair were held the following year.

The town of Salford was granted its charter in about 1230 by Ranulph de Blundeville, Earl of Chester, on behalf of Edward III. Each burgess had a piece of land (burgage) for which he paid rent to the lord of the manor. The burgesses elected an official called the borough-reeve (roughly equivalent to a mayor), and the constables, at the court leet (or 'view of frankpledge').

117

The charter specified the burgesses' rights of pasture; their walls, hedges and ditches had to be kept in good repair. The court leet appointed persons to make sure that dunghills did not cause a problem in the streets. The burgesses' wandering pigs appear to have been regular nuisances even after a swineherd was employed to look after them. Dogs had to be muzzled. The sale of unwholesome meat and fish was frowned upon, and the sale of bread and beer were regulated to make sure that people received their full measure.

The court leet, or 'portmote', also ensured that law and order was maintained, controlled market tolls, oversaw scavenging (cleaning), dealt with criminal matters such as public order offences and supervised the election of the borough-reeve and constables. People were fined ('amerced') if they did not appear at the court leet as requested. The constables' duties and their records are discussed later.

Manchester received its charter in 1301; it was signed by Henry of Trafford, Roger of Pilkington, Adam of Prestwich and others. The charter's provisions were very similar to those in Salford's charter. However, following a dispute in 1359 between John of Gaunt, Duke of Lancaster and Roger de la Warre, a jury decided that Manchester was a market town, not a borough, which meant that only the lord of the manor had the right to exact money from the townsfolk.

The manorial court system for places like Manchester, Worsley and Newton continued until well into the nineteenth century. Some manorial obligations were gradually abolished, however. All of Manchester's residents had to grind their corn and malt at the lord of the manor's mill ('right of soke') on the River Irk. The right of soke regarding corn was repealed by an Act of Parliament in September 1759. The court leet in Manchester finally ceased to exist after Manchester Corporation bought the rights (see Chapter 5), and the court leet's last meeting was held on 15 October 1845.

MANORIAL RECORDS

MCL(M) holds the original court leet records for Manchester (M621), but they are too fragile to be made available to researchers. However, they are available in volume form at the Local Studies reference library. See J.P. Earwaker (ed.), *Court Leet records of the Manor of Manchester*, 12 vols (1884–90), which cover the era 1552–1846 (with gaps). The first four volumes are available on microfilm. See also John Harland (ed.), *A*

Volume of Court Leet Records of the Manor of Manchester in the 16th Century, 2 vols (C.S., 1864–5). The court books for 1687–1731 apparently disappeared early in the nineteenth century.

The manorial court records are a rich source of family names. For example, at the court leet held at Manchester on 30 April 1747, John Walker and James Barnes were fined 10s. each for not serving as jurors. At the same court, the officers and scavengers of St Ann's Square presented Peter Barrow for causing a public nuisance by leaving horse muck in Back Square; he was fined 2s. 6d. (J.P. Earwaker (ed.), *Court Leet records of the Manor of Manchester from the year 1552 to the year 1686, and from the year 1731 to the year 1846*, Vol. VII (Manchester, 1888)).

For Salford's court leet, see J.G. de T. Mandley, *The Portmote or Court Leet Records of the Borough or Town and Royal Manor of Salford from the Year 1597 to the Year 1669 Inclusive* (Chetham Society), vols 46 and 48 (1902) and James Tait (ed.), *Records of some Salford Portmoots in the Sixteenth Century* (Chetham Society, New Series (Second Series)), Vol. 80 (1921).

Manorial estate records may be held by more than one archive. A search on TNA Discovery reveals that the records for Manchester barony (manor) are held by MCL(M), JRL (CLD), LA (DDK, DDX) and TNA (DL 30). The records for Salford manor are held by TNA (DL 30, 32), LA (DDM, DDK) and JRL (CLD). Manors in the Duchy of Lancaster are held by TNA (DL).

The Manorial Documents Register (MDR) is a finding aid to manorial documents for England and Wales arranged by county; it is part of TNA Discovery. Records for manors owned by the Crown and some other manors are kept at TNA; see series SC 2 and DL 30. There's online help for manorial records, www.nationalarchives.gov.uk/help-with-your-research/research-guides/manors-further-research/.

Manors may be mentioned in wills or administration orders, or solicitors' records, because estates changed hands when family members died (if there was no heir) or sometimes by marriage. For example, Barton-upon-Irwell manor was owned by the Barton family until the Booths acquired it in the late thirteenth century. It was later held by the Trafford and Legh families. JRL holds court rolls for Barton-upon-Irwell manor, 1692–1768 (MS295), and LA holds more than thirty collections for this manor (DDTR).

Some manorial records are archived in ecclesiastical collections. The church was a very important landholder and Manchester Cathedral (formerly the Collegiate Church) had vast holdings including the manor of Newton, Deansgate and Kirkmanshulme. The Cathedral's Capitular Records are invaluable for historians (see the archive listing in Chapter 1).

Other types of manorial records you may come across are 'rentals', 'custumals', 'compoti', surveys, 'terriers', maps and 'inquisitions post mortem'. Chris Phillips' website has a detailed guide to medieval records in England for genealogists, www.medievalgenealogy.org.uk/about.shtml.

An 'inquisition post mortem', or 'escheat', was held before a jury if a person who died was a Crown tenant. If there was no heir, the lands reverted to the king. If the heir was under age, they were made a ward of court. The inquisition included the tenant's name and date of death, the manors he or she held (sometimes with names of tenants) and the name and age of the tenant's heir. Inquisitions post mortem can also be found in the Palatine and Duchy of Lancaster court records (see below).

'Mapping the Medieval Countryside' is a major research project which is creating a digital edition of the medieval English inquisitions post mortem from *c*.1236–1509 (currently in beta phase), www.inquisitionspostmortem.ac.uk/.

GREAT ESTATES AND OLD FAMILIES

Several of Manchester's ancient halls have survived to modern times despite spiralling restoration and conservation costs. To give just a few examples, Baguley Hall at Wythenshawe, home of the de Baguley family, dates back to the fourteenth century and is currently awaiting restoration, http://bit.ly/1U5AdlR. Clayton Hall, a rare survival of a moated residence, was home to the Byron family; Humphrey Chetham was later its owner. It's now a museum, www.claytonhall.org/ index.htm.

Platt Hall (now the Gallery of Costume) was home to the Platt family, then the Worsleys; the current building was built during George III's reign by Deborah Carill-Worsley. Sadly, Wythenshawe Hall, the sixteenth-century home of the Tattons of Chester, recently suffered a disastrous fire, www.wythenshawehall.com.

In Salford, Agecroft Hall was the residence of the Langley family, then the Daunteseys and others. In the mid-1920s the hall was bought by an American family, dismantled and shipped lock, stock and barrel

HIC ADIACET CORPVS ANTONIJ MOSLEY

Part of a Mosley family brass, dated 1607, in Manchester Cathedral. Manchester Old and New *(Cassell & Co., c.1894), Vol. II. (Author's collection)*

Ordsall Hall. The building's distinctive 'quatrefoil' panels were plastered over at this date. Alfred Rimmer, Summer Rambles Around Manchester *(John Heywood, n.d., c.1890). (Author's collection)*

to Virginia in the USA, where it still stands. However, Ordsall Hall, the Radclyffe family's home for centuries, was recently restored and is open to the public, www.salfordcommunityleisure.co.uk/culture/ordsall-hall.

The main archives at Manchester, Preston and Salford hold records for many important local families. As with all major collections, a particular family's or estate's papers may be split across several archives, and you should use TNA Discovery to locate them.

MCL(G)'s collections include the Ackers family of Manchester and Salford (E17); the Asshetons of Middleton (E7); the Bagot family's mining interests (E3); the Egertons of Heaton Hall (E4); and the Legh family of Lyme Park (E17). MCL(M) holds records for the Ackers family of Manchester (M159); Bagot family of Middle Hulton's estate papers (L5); the Mosley family (M377), and others.

SCA holds records for the Egerton family (Earls of Bridgewater and Ellesmere – see Chapter 3), the Leigh family of Worsley and the Ormesher family of Eccles (U205). Use GMLives for more information.

LA's vast collections include the Kenyon family of Peel Hall's family papers, 1319–1960 with quarter session, sheriff and assize records, and hearth tax returns (DDKE). The Kay-Shuttleworth family of Gawthorpe Hall's estate papers are in series DDKS, and Kay-Shuttleworth family papers are in series DDX 2123. The de Trafford of Trafford papers, dating from the twelfth to twentieth centuries, include the manors of Barton, Mawdesley and Stretford (DDTR). The Hulton of Hulton archive, c.1190–1998 includes estates in Manchester, Ordsall and Salford; the Hopwood manuscripts, 1337–1825 also include Manchester and Salford. For the Stanley family (Earls of Derby) collection, 1235–1892, see DDK. The Slater, Heelis & Co. (Manchester solicitors) collection, 1648–1973 includes the Ackers family muniments and records for places in Manchester and Salford.

The Manchester UK website has a list of old families in northwest England, http://www.manchester2002-uk.com/history/old-families2.html.

If your ancestors had noble blood, or were upwardly mobile, then their family tree probably appeared in publications like Burke's *Peerage and Baronetage* (1826 onwards) or Debrett's Peerage. The Society of Genealogists Library has a collection of peerages and publications such as *Kelly's Handbook to the Titled, Landed and Official Classes* (1880 onwards). For Lancashire, see J. Croston, *The County Families of*

Lancashire and Cheshire (John Heywood, 1887), which includes the Mosley, Hulton and Trafford families.

The College of Arms is the official repository for coats of arms and pedigrees in England and Wales, www.college-of-arms.gov.uk/. The Heraldry Society also has information on family pedigrees and coats-of-arms, www.theheraldrysociety.com/home.htm. Burke's Peerage has an online database (subscription needed), www.burkespeerage.com/search.php. The Peerage website is free and has surname indexes: www.thepeerage.com.

The 'visitations' of the royal heralds to Lancashire in the early sixteenth and seventeenth centuries can prove useful if your ancestor was blue-blooded. The royal heralds monitored which families had the right to bear arms. After interviewing the families, they recorded pedigrees for them. The publications of the historic and antiquarian societies for Lancashire and Cheshire often include detailed family trees and pedigrees.

LAW AND ORDER
Policing Manchester and Salford Before Incorporation
Manchester and Salford had no professional police force for many centuries. In each manor or township, the borough-reeve and his constables were responsible for keeping law and order, and as already mentioned, they were appointed by the court leet.

In Manchester the two constables had a deputy-constable and a beadle to help them carry out their duties; the latter two officials received a salary. The beadle was a notable figure, splendidly dressed in a gown and cap with a gold fringe and lace, and scarlet stockings. The beadle and constables carried truncheons adorned with the town's coat of arms and a silver mount.

The constables ensured that punishments were carried out for misdemeanours. People were put in the stocks, made to stand in the pillory or whipped (males and females). Women offenders would be ducked in the pond or made to wear a 'scold's bridle' and paraded before the townsfolk. Night watchmen were employed to patrol the streets at night, and some primitive precautions were taken against fire. The constables also presented people to the court for gambling, fighting and drunkenness. Suspicious persons were arrested and homeless people moved on.

Policing the refractory working classes was not always easy. In 1796, when a constable went to Newton to serve an arrest warrant, the locals made him eat the offending document and sent him packing. See Eric J. Hewitt, *Capital of Discontent: Crime and Protest in Manchester's Industrial Revolution* (History Press, 2014) and Don Hale, *Manchester Thief-takers* (Bridge Books, 2007).

Local magistrates were responsible for keeping the peace. They issued warrants and read the Riot Act when necessary (i.e. ordered a disorderly meeting to disperse). When trouble seemed imminent (as at Peterloo) lots of 'special' constables were enrolled, and magistrates requested troops to act 'in aid of the civil power'.

MCL has copies of J.P. Earwaker (ed.), *The Constables' Accounts for the Manor of Manchester*, 3 vols (Blacklock, 1891–2), which covers the era 1612–1776 (with some gaps). According to Earwaker, shortly after Manchester Corporation bought the manorial rights in 1845, some constables' accounts were sold as waste paper! Luckily, a volume was rescued.

MCL(M) holds the Manchester borough-reeve's papers, 1649–1848 (M91). This collection includes a minute book of the Act of Parliament Committee for a new Police Bill, 1823–30; other committees, 1828–30; constables' accounts, 1613–48, 1743–85; proceedings of public meetings appointed by the borough-reeve and constables, 1821–38; Poor Law papers and early constables' papers. Another collection of borough-reeve's and constables' papers, 1806–38 includes taxation records, 1831–4, public health 1831–7, law and order, 1826–34 and papers relating to organizing public events (M71).

Policing Manchester and Salford After Incorporation

The Municipal Corporations Act (1835) gave corporations powers to set up a Watch Committee. Manchester's first Chief Constable was Captain Edward Willis. However, as discussed in Chapter 5, it was not until 1843 that Manchester Corporation took over the police commissioners' role.

By 1849 Manchester City Police had over 400 officers and men, including 370 constables; Salford had 40 officers and men. That year Manchester police arrested over 4,600 persons (650 were committed for trial), and Salford police took into custody over 1,600 persons (149 were committed for trial). During the nineteenth century, a significant proportion of those arrested and later hanged for murder were of Irish origin, many of whom were apparently the worse for drink at the time of their offence.

The first Manchester City policeman killed on duty was Police Sergeant Charles Brett. He was shot during a famous incident in September 1867 when some Fenian (Irish nationalist) prisoners were rescued from a police van while in transit. Over two-dozen Irishmen were arrested following the incident. Three Irishmen (the 'Manchester Martyrs') were found guilty of murder and hanged from a temporary gallows in front of the New Bailey prison.

There was a county wide force as well as the local police forces: the Lancashire County Constabulary was founded in 1840. Manchester City Police and Salford City Police amalgamated in 1968; this body merged with Lancashire Constabulary when the county boundaries changed in 1974 to form Greater Manchester Police.

LA has minute books for the Lancashire Constabulary Committee, 1840–89, Manchester Division charge books, 1842–54 and 1894–5, and summons books, 1847–54 and 1859–62 (QEV). It also has a Manchester Division Stretford section charge book, 1939–43 (PLA 47/1), and a 1923 Manchester City Police instruction book (PLA 18/11).

If your ancestor worked for Lancashire County Constabulary, you can search an online database, 1840–1925: http://www3.lancashire.gov.uk/education/record_office/records/policesearch.asp.

Findmypast's Manchester Collection includes the Manchester City Police Index, 1812–1941, which has over 10,600 entries. The appointment registers in this collection include the policeman's age, place of birth, religion, trade, marital status, physical description and career history. Members of MLFHS can access this index via the society's website. There's an online guide to police archives in England and Wales by Ian Bridgeman and Clive Emsley, http://bit.ly/2fhF0CI.

Greater Manchester Police Museum and Archives

The museum has displays on the history of policing in Manchester. The archive holds personnel service records for police officers, including personal memorabilia (only for the Greater Manchester area), police manuals and handbooks, and administrative records for police forces prior to 1974. The archive's collections also include the Aliens Register for Salford, 1914–69 with some gaps. (The Manchester Aliens Register is no longer extant.) The museum has copies of the *Police Gazette* on microfilm, 1839–1900 (some gaps), www.gmpmuseum.co.uk/.

The website has a roll of honour (with photos) from the 1800s to the present day for policemen and women in the Greater Manchester area who lost their lives while on duty, www.gmpmuseum.co.uk/roll-of-honour/. The Greater Manchester Police Museum does not hold prison records; see the separate section below. Archive visits by appointment only; an initial research enquiry is free but a fee is payable for some services.

Prisons and Prison Records

From Tudor times until the late eighteenth century, the House of Correction at Hunt's Bank in Manchester was used as the prison for Salford Hundred. Its original purpose was to confine papist recusants. There was also a dungeon on Salford Old Bridge, as noted earlier.

In 1787, the first stone of the New Bailey Prison and Courthouse at Salford was laid by Thomas Butterworth Bayley. The New Bailey opened three years later; it had a House of Correction attached to it. Prisoners wore a blue and red uniform before their trial, and blue and yellow after their conviction. During the 1830s a daily court was held there by the police magistrate for Manchester and Salford. The borough of Manchester had no prison of its own, so short-stay prisoners were kept in New Bailey Prison; long-stay prisoners were sent to the county gaol in Lancaster Castle.

During the eighteenth century, persons were sometimes hanged on the spot where they committed the offence. In 1790 a man called Macnamara was hanged for burglary on Kersal Moor. However, convicted felons were usually hanged at Lancaster, www.lancastercastle.com/executions-in-lancaster-1801-1910. TNA holds records for Lancaster county gaol (PCOM); LA has copies on microfilm.

New Bailey Prison introduced the 'silent system' (in which people were not permitted to speak to one another) in 1834. Prisoners also worked on the treadwheel, and sand-mill (known as the 'crank'). Some prisoners learnt weaving and shoemaking.

A new prison was built at Belle Vue (Hyde Road) in Manchester c.1845, but it proved too small, and some prisoners were still sent to the New Bailey. Belle Vue closed in 1888 and was demolished a few years later. Strangeways Prison on Southall Street was built to replace the

New Bailey, which closed in 1868. Strangeways served as the jail for the whole of Salford Hundred. It had a gallows, and the Capital Punishment website lists some executed felons, www.capitalpunishmentuk.org/strangeway.html.

A full list of surviving male and female prisoner records held by MLIA for New Bailey, Belle Vue and Strangeways is available on GMLives (M600). Findmypast's Manchester Collection has prison registers for New Bailey Prison, Salford, 1847–72 (some gaps); Belle Vue, 1850–80 (gaps); and Strangeways, 1867–81 (gaps). Gerard Lodge's website has a great deal of information on Manchester courts and prisons, www.manchester-family-history-research.co.uk/.

Criminal registers list people indicted for offences, the assize or quarter sessions court where the case was heard and the verdict. Check these registers first if you do not know where a prisoner was tried. Criminal registers and prisoners' registers are kept at TNA, which has an online guide to crime and punishment, www.national archives.gov.uk/help-with-your-research/research-guides/crime-and-punishment/.

The Duchy of Lancaster and the Palatinate Courts

In 1351 Henry, fourth Earl of Lancaster, was granted palatine powers by Edward III and given the title of first Duke of Lancaster. In effect Lancashire became Henry's own personal kingdom, although taxes were paid to the Crown. Henry chose his own sheriff, judges and magistrates for the civil and criminal courts in the county palatine. The palatine lapsed briefly but after 1399 the Duchy of Lancaster, and palatinate powers, belonged to the Crown. However, the palatine still held separate courts from the king's courts. The palatine courts were administered by the Duchy, which had its own court, the Court of Duchy Chamber. The Duke of Lancaster (i.e. the Crown) appointed the county sheriff and chancellor; the latter appointed local magistrates and other officers.

TNA's Palatinate records (PL) include many court records, including chancery court and administration records, court of common pleas, equity cases, etc. The series listing on TNA Discovery has more information, http://discovery.nationalarchives.gov.uk/details/r/C228/.

DUCHY AND COUNTY PALATINE COURT OF CHANCERY, MANCHESTER DISTRICT REGISTRY

Manchester had its own District Registrar for the Court of Chancery from 1857, and these records are held at TNA as follows:

• Case Files including summonses, affidavits, estate administration, probate disputes, orders, petitions, writs, statements of claim, copy orders, bills, etc. Others include actions concerning landlords and tenants, probate problems, guardianships of minors, mortgages, partnerships, patents and designs, tenancies, trademarks, etc., 1871–1972 (with some gaps after 1920) (PL 31).
• Cause Books (wills and probate) concerning cases registered and heard at Manchester, 1853–1922 (PL 38).
• Companies' winding-up files including petitions, accounts, orders, affidavits, creditors' proofs of debts, liquidators' bills of costs, receivers' reports, etc., 1892–1952 (PL 32).
• Entry books of decrees and orders (many relating to disputed wills or business problems), 1857–1922 (PL 34).
• Registrar's Orders, 1857–77 (PL 42).
• Reports and certificates, taxation, trusteeships, receivers' accounts and funds administered by the Chancery Court following a court order; some certificates relate to estates and properties, etc., 1855–1968 (thirty-year closure) (PL 41).

Some parts of Manchester and Salford were (and still are) within the jurisdiction of the Duchy of Lancaster. TNA holds a large collection of records, which contains over fifty series, for the Duchy of Lancaster, including the Court of Duchy Chamber, http://discovery.national archives.gov.uk/details/r/C83. The main series include pleadings, entry books (for equity pleadings), affidavits, certificates, reports and petitions; sealed depositions (for equity pleadings); royal charters, and papers in lawsuits. Online indexes with surnames are available for some Duchy Chamber series.

LA's collections include Duchy and Palatine records relating to the assizes, chancery and local estates (see Table 6 opposite). More information can be found on the LA Online Catalogue, LANCAT.

Table 6: Duchy of Lancaster and Palatine Court Records at Lancashire Archives

Record Type	Dates Covered	Series Refs
Assize rolls (Duchy of Lancaster)	1664, 1667–9, 1672–3	PPLC 2/1–6
Assize rolls (Palatine)	Nineteenth century	DDCM/1
Chancery	1947–71	PPLC/3
Palatinate records	1664–twentieth century	PPLC

Salford Court of the Hundred (Wapentake)

This ancient court dated back to Anglo-Saxon times. In the early fifteenth century, the Earls of Sefton (Molyneux family) became the hereditary high stewards of this court. Its court rolls can be found at LA (DDM7).

At the start of the nineteenth century, the Salford Hundred Court was limited to civil claims less than 40s. (£2); it met every three weeks. (It should not be confused with the Salford Court Leet, which met twice a year at the Town Hall until at least the late 1850s). Claims over £2 were heard at the Court of Queen's Bench, or at the Court of Common Pleas at Preston.

In Manchester a Court of Record was founded in 1845 for claims under £20; it met at Brown Street. The court for Salford Hundred was extended in 1862 to become a Court of Record for claims up to £50 (for the whole Hundred except the City of Manchester). It was held at Salford Town Hall until the new Assize Courts were built at Strangeways. In 1868 an Act of Parliament merged the City of Manchester Court of Record with Salford Hundred Court, which continued in existence until 1971.

Many early records for the court were destroyed during the Manchester Blitz in the Second World War. SCA holds Salford Hundred Court records, 1828–67 (L/HJ). MCL(M) has records for Salford Hundred Court of Record, 1845–1971 including rules of Manchester Borough Court of Record and Salford Hundred Court of Record, 1845–1971; government inquiries, 1911–1969; administrative papers, 1852–1956; papers concerning court officials, 1858–1926; names of those serving the court from the 1830s to 1964; business of the court, 1916–71 including the names of those appearing in court, etc. (M123).

Manchester County Court and Salford County Court were formed in 1846 to deal with small civil claims (initially up to £20; later £50), but no records are seemingly extant.

Assize Courts

Assize courts dealt with the most serious criminal offences. Manchester and Salford were not part of the assize circuit; assizes and common pleas were held by the Palatine Court at Lancaster twice yearly. After 1835 there was an additional court sitting at Salford for the whole Hundred, and at Liverpool for West Derby Hundred, but the time of year varied. In 1876 the Palatine Court at Lancaster was superseded by the Assizes Northern Circuit. Assize records for Manchester and Salford are held by LA and TNA (see Tables 6, previous page, and 7, opposite).

Crown minute books record the business of each court session, often with names of jurors, names of prisoners tried, their offences, verdicts and sentences; 'order books' detail sentences given by judges against convicts (with name, offence and sentence). Assize rolls may include names of persons convicted, orders for the commutation of death sentences to transportation, names of magistrates, court correspondence, depositions, jury lists and copies of the court records, etc.

It became increasingly inconvenient for Manchester and Salford people to have to travel a long way to get their cases heard. Splendid new Gothic-style Assize Courts were built on Great Ducie Street, Strangeways, and after 1868 additional assizes for Salford Hundred were held there (a Crown court and civil court). Greater Manchester Police Museum holds Calendars of Prisoners for the Assize Court of Manchester, 1882–1964 (with gaps).

When Manchester Crown Court was founded in 1956, it took over the quarter sessions and assizes work at Manchester, and also Salford's assize work. MCL(M) holds two volumes of calendars of prisoners for Manchester Crown Court, 1956–60 (M545). TNA holds case files, 1971–96 (J 287) and indictments, 1972–5 (J 288) for Manchester Crown Court.

Table 7: Key to Assizes for Lancashire, 1559–1971 at
The National Archives

Type of Record	Dates	Series Refs
Bills of Costs	1947–71	ASSI 93
Civil minute books (nisi prius)	1877–1971	ASSI 54
Crown minute and Gaol Books	1524–1843	PL 25
Crown minute and Gaol Books	1686–1877	PL 28
Depositions	1663–1867	PL 27
Depositions	1877–1971	ASSI 52
Estreats (returns of penalties)	1843–90	ASSI 46
Indictments (and some coroners' files)	1660–1867	PL 26
Indictments	1877–1971	ASSI 51
Medical and probation reports*	1946–57	ASSI 86
Order books	1736–1848	PL 28
Order books	1879–1924	ASSI 53

* Closed for seventy-five years.

Quarter and Petty Sessions

Lesser criminal offences and day-to-day law enforcement were dealt with by magistrates at quarter sessions, held four times a year. Prior to 1839, cases for Manchester and Salford were heard at quarter sessions for Salford Hundred at Lancaster Castle. After Manchester was incorporated as a borough, it held its own quarter sessions at Brown Street.

Over the years, both towns' growing population led to 'petty' sessions for minor offences and juvenile delinquency in order to reduce the amount of court business at quarter sessions. For example, the police and magistrates' courts were kept extremely busy in the late 1890s by the so-called 'scuttling menace', when rival gang wars broke out in Manchester and Salford. See Andrew Davies, *The Gangs Of Manchester* (Milo Press, 2009).

LA hold quarter sessions records, 1583–1999 (Q); calendars of prisoners tried at quarter sessions and assizes, 1801–1967 (QJC); petty sessions, 1583–1972 (QS); petitions including gaol accounts, calendars of prisoners and appointments of constables (QSP); and annual sessions proceedings and reports (QSZ).

MCL(M) holds calendars of prisoners tried at Lancashire Quarter Sessions (Hundred of Salford), 1808–47 (L27). This series includes calendars of all the prisoners in New Bailey prison, 1821–47 (L27/2). For Borough/City of Manchester Quarter Sessions Court records, including calendars of prisoners, 1839–1951, see series M116. MCL also has copies of session order books for the Lancashire Quarter Sessions, 1626–1888 on microfilm.

MCL(M) holds records for the City of Manchester Petty Sessions, 1839–1970 (M117). This series includes convictions, court registers, summons, licences, etc. Petty sessions were also held at Manchester for areas outside the cities of Manchester and Salford.

Salford Magistrates' Court in the Town Hall on Bexley Square opened in 1840. The quarter sessions for Salford Borough were held there, and after 1890 Salford City held its own quarter sessions there, too. The court closed in 2011. MCL(G) holds records for Salford City Quarter Sessions, including calendars of prisoners, indictments, depositions, etc., 1890–1971 (ASQS). Records for this body after 1971 are held at Manchester and Salford Magistrates' Court.

Publicans and Public Houses

The 'demon drink' was the cause of many social problems and disorder. Manchester and Salford folk enjoyed a tipple, and the area was well-stocked with public houses, alehouses and breweries. According to one estimate, Manchester had over 1,850 beer-houses, gin-shops and pubs for its 460,400 souls in the 1830s. Salford's gin-palaces were brilliantly lit by gaslight, and would have seemed a tempting prospect to workers after a hard day's graft.

A person could not run a pub unless the local magistrates had certified that he was trustworthy. Quarter sessions and Watch Committee records often include victuallers' licences, registers of licences, recognizance rolls and certificates of good character. See Jeremy Gibson, *Victuallers' Licences: Records for Family and Local Historians* (3rd edn) (Family History Partnership, 2009). The Pub History Society website has a good overview of sources for researchers, www.pubhistorysociety.co.uk.

Coroners' Records

If a person suffered from a sudden, unexplained or suspicious death, then the coroner held an inquest. From the late fifteenth century to the mid-eighteenth century, coroners' inquest records were given to the assize judges, who in turn passed them to the court of the King's Bench (KB at TNA). After 1752, coroners' inquests were filed at quarter sessions, so surviving records are held locally. TNA has a research guide to coroners' inquisitions (inquests): www.nationalarchives.gov.uk/help-with-your-research/research-guides/coroners-inquests/.

The Lancaster coroner held inquests for Manchester persons before 1839. After incorporation, Manchester borough appointed its own coroner. The Lancaster coroner held inquests for Salford persons up to 1889, when Salford became a county borough. Records for the Salford Borough Coroner do not appear to have survived prior to 1912.

After Salford became a city in 1926, the office was re-named Salford City Coroner. However, there was also a Salford County Coroner who was responsible for Eccles, Swinton and Pendlebury, Irlam and Worsley. Following the creation of Greater Manchester in 1974, the Bolton Coroner was given jurisdiction for the City of Salford.

Local newspapers are the best source of information about inquests, which were often reported in detail, and the nature and cause of death given, and other family members sometimes mentioned.

Inquest records mostly only give limited information such as the verdict. Associated records may include lists of coroners' expenses. Surviving records for the Lancaster coroner are held by LA (QSP). For coroners' files for the Duchy of Lancaster, see DL 46, JUST 1 and JUST 3 at TNA.

Only a small number of coroners' records survive for Manchester and Salford, and they are closed for seventy-five years, except for exceptional circumstances. Table 8 overleaf lists the relevant series at Manchester and Preston. Indexes of inquests are available for the Manchester Coroner's Court. The information listed includes the deceased's name; date of death; date of inquest; where and when inquest held; officer in charge of case; age of deceased; address of deceased; and place of death, cause of death, etc.

One rare survival is a series of witness depositions for Manchester Coroner's inquests from 22 August 1851 to 24 December 1852 (M381/1/1/1–2 at MCL(G)). Gerard Lodge has compiled an index, www.manchester-family-history-research.co.uk/new_page_36.htm.

Table 8: Coroners' Records

Coroner's Office	Archive	Ref.	Dates Covered
Bolton Coroner	MCL(G)	A1	1961–2009
Lancaster Coroner	LA	QSP	1648–1908
Manchester Coroner depositions	MCL(M)	M381	1851–2
Manchester Coroner inquests and post-mortems	MCL(G)	A2	1959–2007
Manchester Coroner inquests indexes	MCL(G)	A2	1914–96
Manchester Coroner news cuttings	MCL(M)	M381	1900–38
Salford Borough Coroner	MCL(G)	A.QSC	1912–25
Salford City Coroner	MCL(G)	A.QSC	1932–5, 1937–74
Salford County Coroner	LA	CR13	1925–71

LOCAL AND NATIONAL TAXATION

The Crown and governments have levied taxes since time immemorial. The Exchequer series at TNA includes records of taxation and other monies collected for Lancashire. See sheriffs' accounts (E 199); exchequer pipe rolls are in E 372. For clerical taxes, see E 179, E 331–E 344 and E 347. Taxation records, 1640–1822 include hearth taxes, lay subsidy rolls, poll taxes, pensions, land tax, estate taxes and much more for Lancashire (E 179). See also James Tait (ed.), *Taxation in Salford Hundred 1524–1802*, CS, New Series (Second Series), Vol. 83, 1924. This work includes a transcript of returns for lay subsidies, the hearth tax and land taxes, 1780–1802.

Sometimes lists of residents were compiled for various administrative purposes. One of the earliest examples for Salford Hundred is a list of gentlemen 'of the best calling' who lent money to the Crown in 1588, the year of the Spanish Armada. This list includes Sir Edmund Trafford, George Pilkington and John Molyneux (*Chetham*

Miscellanies, Old Series 57, Vol. 3, 1862). The same volume also contains a 'Pole' Book dated 22 May 1690. This was a poll tax (not an electoral register) to raise money for the war effort with France. The Poll Book lists the inhabitants street by street and mentions if they were Catholic. The borough-reeve's records at MCL(M) include papers relating to several taxes levied during the seventeenth century (M91).

Freeholders' lists can be useful, too as they give name, address and occupation. For LA's collection of freeholders' lists (1696–1832: those qualified to serve on juries), see QDF.

Rate Books

Businesses and householders paid rates. Rate books are a good way of establishing the location of a person or firm over several years, especially if you are struggling to find them in the census (in particular the 1851 'unfilmed' census for Manchester). The books are organized by address, not surname. See the listings of township records (Tables 3 and 5) in Chapter 5 for Manchester and Salford, and also the sections on corporation records.

MCL has copies of Manchester rate books, 1706–1901 on microfilm; however, some years are lost, or are incomplete. Copies of rate books from 1902–57 can be viewed by appointment in the search room (two weeks' notice is required). An online guide is available, http://bit.ly/2hDAzVn.

SCA has lists of ratepayers or electors for Salford township for 1817, for some years between 1819 and 1834, and for the years 1841–2 on microfilm. SCA also has three petitions dated 1843 listing names of ratepayers in Salford, Pendlebury and Pendleton townships (U349/01–3).

Findmypast's Manchester Collection of rate books for 1706–1900 includes several of the smaller townships. Members of MLFHS can access a database of owners and occupiers for over 7,500 properties in the Chorlton-upon-Medlock Poor Rate Book for 1851, as well as another list for 500 properties in the Pendlebury Poor Rate Book for 1852, via the society's website.

Land Taxes and Tithes

Land taxes and tithe maps are vital if you are researching land use, farming and agriculture. Quarter sessions records include land tax assessments, for example, LA's collections include land tax assessments for Salford Hundred, 1780–1832 (QDL/S). In 1873, a 'census' of everyone who owned at least 1 acre of land was taken for Lancashire. See the House of Commons parliamentary paper, *Returns of Owners of*

Land 1873, Vol. 1, LXXII, Pt. 1, pp. 611–90. A searchable index of the Land Tax Returns is available via Ancestry.

The so-called 'Domesday' land survey took place in 1910. MCL(G) holds Land Tax Valuation Registers for 1910 (A11); unfortunately, each register is arranged in order of property number and street, not surname. The registers have a street index, however. This collection covers Manchester and Salford. MCL(M) has a collection of working maps made during the survey (M76).

Tithe maps are extremely detailed. In 1836 the Tithe Commutation Act enabled people to pay ecclesiastical tithes in cash instead of payment in kind. Where the Act was implemented, accurate maps were made of each parish's land, and the landowners and tenants noted. Some parishes converted to money payments before the Act, so they were not covered by the legislation. Three copies were made of each map and tithe apportionment record; one for the parish chest, one for the tithe commissioners and one for the diocesan register office.

TNA holds the commissioners' copies of tithe maps (IR 29, 30). LA holds tithe maps for the Diocese of Manchester (DRM). LA's online catalogue has a tithes index which includes Manchester and Salford: use the 'advanced search' option and search by 'tithe apportionment', www.lancashire.gov.uk/libraries-and-archives/archives-and-record-office/search-the-archives/lancat.aspx.

See Eric J. Evans and Alan G. Crosby, *Tithes: Maps, Apportionments and the 1836 Act: a guide for local historians* (3rd edn) (British Association for Local History, 1997) and Roger J.P. Kain and Richard R. Oliver, *The Tithe Maps of England and Wales: A Cartographic Analysis and County-by-County Catalogue* (repr. Cambridge University Press, 2011). The Genealogist has an searchable online collection of tithe maps, https://www.thegenealogist.co.uk/tithe/.

During the eighteenth and nineteenth centuries, hundreds of acres of common land and waste were enclosed. Enclosure awards include detailed maps or surveys of the land to be enclosed. For holdings at LA, see *A Handlist of Lancashire Enclosure Acts and Awards* (Lancashire County Council, 1946).

FURTHER READING
Buckley, Angela, *The Real Sherlock Holmes: The Hidden Story of Jerome Caminada*, Pen & Sword, 2014

Caminada, Jerome, *Twenty-Five Years of Detective Life*, London, 1895

Castor, Helen, *The King, the Crown and the Duchy of Lancaster*, Oxford University Press, 2000

Croston, James, *County Families of Lancashire and Cheshire*, London, 1887

'E.P.', *Handbook to the Manchester Assize Courts*, John Heywood, *c.*1864

De Lacy, Margaret, *Prison Reform in Lancashire 1700–1850*, Chetham Society, 1968

Farrer, W. (ed.), *Some Court Rolls of the Lordships, Wapentakes, and Demesne Manors of Thomas, Earl of Lancaster, for the 17th and 18th years of the Reign of Edward II, AD 1323–4*, Vol. XLI, Lancashire and Cheshire Record Society, 1901

Farrer, W. (ed.), *The Lancashire Pipe Rolls of 31 Henry I., A.D. 1130, and of the reigns of Henry II., A.D. 1155–1189; Richard I., A.D. 1189–1199; and King John, A.D. 1199–1216*, Liverpool, 1902

Fielding, Steve, *Hanged At Manchester*, History Press, 2008

Gooderson, Philip, 'Terror on the Streets of Late Victorian Salford and Manchester: The Scuttling Menace', *Manchester Region History Review*, Vol. 11, 1997, pp. 3–11

Harland, John (ed.), *Mamecestre, Being Chapters from the Early Recorded History of the Barony*, Chetham Society, 1861

Hawkings, David T., *Criminal Ancestors*, 2nd edn, History Press, 2009

Kenyon, Denise, *The Origins of Lancashire*, Manchester University Press, 1991

McLynn, Frank, *Crime and Punishment In Eighteenth Century England*, Routledge, 2002

Martinez, A.J., 'Palatinate administration and local society in the palatinate of Lancashire under the Lancastrian kings, 1399–1461', *THSC*, Vol. 156, 2008, pp. 1–25

Midwinter, E.C., *Law and Order in Early Victorian Lancashire*, Borthwick Papers No. 34, York, 1968

Oates, Jonathan, *Tracing Your Ancestors From 1066 to 1837*, Pen & Sword, 2012

Rose, Paul, *The Manchester Martyrs*, Laurence & Wishart, 1970

Somerville, Robert, *History of the Duchy of Lancaster*, London, 1953

Stuart, Denis, *Manorial Records*, Phillimore & Co. Ltd, 2010

Tait, James, *Mediaeval Manchester and the Beginnings of Lancashire*, Manchester University Press, 1904

Wade, Stephen, *Tracing Your Criminal Ancestors*, Pen & Sword, 2009

Chapter 8

WE, THE PEOPLE

NATIONAL CENSUSES, 1801–1911

Censuses and electoral registers are all excellent ways of exploring your family tree for the years between the records of births or baptisms, marriages, burials or deaths.

From 1801 the government took decennial censuses of Britain's population. The 1801–31 censuses were basic head counts of the people in each parish. The 1841 census was the first enumeration to give an address for each household, the names of everyone in the household, their age, occupation and place of origin (in or outside the county, Scotland, Ireland or abroad). This census should be used with caution, however, for calculating dates of birth as the ages of persons over 15 years old were 'rounded down' to the nearest five years. The censuses from 1851 onwards give more accurate ages and more details on each person's place of origin. See Peter Christian and David Annal, *Census: The Family Historian's Guide* (A. & C. Black, 2014) and Emma Jolly, *Tracing Your Ancestors Using The Census* (Pen & Sword, 2013).

Manchester and Salford family historians face a potential problem. The 1851 census returns for several registration districts in Manchester, Chorlton, Salford, etc., were damaged in a near disastrous flood in London. They were too badly damaged to be copied on to microfilm and the details of over 217,000 people in the affected areas were illegible. The records for Blackley, Harpurhey and Moston were lost forever, along with parts of Hulme, St George's and the London Road district.

In the early 1990s, MLFHS began a volunteer project to transcribe the surviving records which were still readable but too fragile to film. After fourteen years of work, 82 per cent of the missing census enumerations were recovered. The 'Unfilmed' 1851 Census website has a free searchable street index and surname index, www.1851-unfilmed.org.uk.

The easiest way to search the 1841–1911 censuses for Manchester and Salford is via the main genealogy suppliers. As noted earlier, Ancestry and Findmypast census records (transcripts and images) are free to access via MCC library computers. Each supplier has different name indexes, so if you cannot find your ancestor via one supplier, it's worth searching the others. Findmypast also has a free searchable index to MLFHS's un-filmed 1851 census transcripts. In a separate project, using new illumination techniques, Ancestry has digitized and indexed the original damaged enumeration books. The Ancestry index is not as complete as Findmypast's, but you can see images of the damaged documents – useful if you want to check the information yourself.

Members of MLFHS can access a street index for Manchester and Salford for the 1841 census, with original Home Office references and enumeration districts, via the society's website. Members can also access full transcripts of the damaged 1851 census returns for Manchester and Salford via the society's website. The society's online bookshop sells CD-ROMs of the 1851 transcripts, as well as CD-ROMs of street and surname indexes for the 1891 censuses for Salford and Manchester.

The censuses for 1841–1901 can also be viewed at SLHL; card indexes are available. Please note that the 1921 census will not be released until 2022, and the 1931 census records were destroyed in a fire during WW2. Another type of 'census', National Registration, is discussed below.

RADICAL MANCHESTER AND SALFORD

Manchester was in the forefront of political change. The roll-call of the city's battles for people's rights is an honourable one: Peterloo, Chartism, trade unionism, 'Votes for Women', to name just a few.

In the late eighteenth century the franchise was limited to the landed gentry and those with a limited property qualification. The working classes had no vote. There was also growing frustration among the middle classes that large towns like Manchester and Salford had no MP. (Manchester briefly had an MP during the Commonwealth; burgesses elected an MP in 1654 and 1656, but the town lost its MP with the Restoration.) If Manchester was not represented in Parliament, its merchants could not lobby effectively on important issues affecting their trade and industry.

Thomas Paine's *Rights of Man* (1791–2) pioneered the idea of democracy, and Mancunian Thomas Walker was one of the leading lights in the fight for parliamentary reform. However, the French Revolution virtually nipped in the bud this incipient movement. The authorities viewed those who promoted reform as potential revolutionaries. Spies and informers were paid to spy on Radicals like Walker, who was arrested and tried (but acquitted) for attempting to overthrow the constitution.

The long war with France led to great hardship in the manufacturing districts. 'Hampden Clubs', which promoted parliamentary reform and universal suffrage, sprang up all over the UK. Silk weaver Samuel Bamford was secretary of the Middleton club. The Blanketeers' march of 1817 was an attempt by starving weavers to present a petition to the Prince Regent, but it was swiftly dispersed by the army and constables.

'Manchester Bull Hunt'. A bull, with the head of John Bull, tossing a member of the Manchester Yeomanry and attacking a magistrate. Behind the bull is a group of reformers led by Henry Hunt holding a paper inscribed 'Coron[er's] Inquest'. (Courtesy Library of Congress LC-USZC4-6857)

The Peterloo Massacre

Several meetings in favour of parliamentary reform were held at St Peter's Field in 1818 and 1819. When local magistrates discovered that a mass meeting was to be held in August 1819, and that leading Radical Henry Hunt was to address the people, they feared the worst.

On 16 August 1819, an estimated 60–80,000 people – men, women and children – assembled on St Peter's Field waiting to hear the famous Henry Hunt. It was a sunny day, and the crowd was in holiday mood.

The magistrates had several hundred special constables stationed in a number of locations. The 15th Hussars (cavalry), the 88th and 31st Foot (infantry), the Royal Horse Artillery, the Manchester and Salford Yeomanry Cavalry, and the Cheshire Yeomanry were also on standby in case of trouble.

Unfortunately, the Manchester magistrates were completely unnerved by the immense size of the crowd. Convinced that a major insurrection was planned, they panicked, and requested the town's deputy constable, Joseph Nadin, to arrest Hunt with the aid of troops.

The Manchester and Salford Yeomanry, and Nadin, tried to force their way through the tightly packed crowd. The cavalrymen's horses became frightened and the Yeomanry began to slash their way through. As people tried to flee, and more troops arrived, the magistrates grew convinced that the crowd was attacking the soldiers. They asked the officer in charge of the Hussars to clear the field. In the ensuing melee between 11 and 15 people died and at least 400 people, about a quarter of which were women, were injured. The reformers arrested at Peterloo – Henry Hunt, Samuel Bamford and others – were incarcerated in Salford's New Bailey Prison.

The 'Manchester Meeting', nicknamed 'Peterloo' in an ironic reference to Waterloo, was a pivotal event in Radical history. It led the government to crack down on political meetings and societies, and reform stalled for several years. A plaque marks the site of Peterloo, and there is a campaign for a permanent memorial.

Many books have been published on the events leading up to Peterloo and its aftermath. See, for example, Samuel Bamford, *Passages In the Life Of A Radical*, 2 vols (Simpkin, Marshall & Co., 1844); F.A. Bruton (ed.), *Three Accounts of Peterloo* (Manchester University Press, 1921); Joyce Marlow, *The Peterloo Massacre* (Readers Union, 1969); D. Read, *Peterloo: The Massacre and Its Background* (Manchester

University Press, 1958); and Archibald Prentice, *Historical Sketches and Personal Recollections of Manchester* (2nd edn), (Manchester, 1851).

MLIA holds some memoirs and contemporary accounts of Peterloo. CL has a subscriptions list for the relief of special constables (one from Manchester was killed on the day) (A.2.14). JRL holds an account book for the relief of 350 victims (MS172).

The Working Class Movement Library has a wealth of material about Peterloo, including pamphlets by Radical printer James Wroe listing those killed and injured, www.wcml.org.uk/our-collections/protest-politics-and-campaigning-for-change/peterloo-massacre/. The People's History Museum has displays and contemporary prints about the fight for democracy, and a rare Peterloo handkerchief depicting the massacre, www.phm.org.uk/our-collection/peterloo-handkerchief/.

Chartism

The 1832 Reform Act (see below) greatly disappointed many campaigners for reform as their dream had not been achieved. In the late 1830s, growing frustration among the working classes led to the birth of Chartism. The reformers' 'six-point Charter' demanded universal male suffrage; annual parliaments; vote by secret ballot; the abolition of the property qualification for MPs; payment for MPs; and equal electoral districts. The movement had its own newspaper, the *Northern Star*, which was extremely popular.

The movement was taken up with enthusiasm in Manchester and Salford, and on 24 September 1838 a mass meeting was held at Kersal Moor. Four years later, the Chartists took direct action in the 'Plug Plot' strikes. Factories were brought to a standstill when strikers removed the plugs from the mill boilers. Workers marched on Manchester, but were dispersed by troops.

The Oldham Road and Ancoats districts of Manchester were particular Chartist strongholds, and in August 1848, 300 policemen swooped and arrested 15 people. However, the movement suffered from weak leadership, and its lack of success in achieving reform, combined with government suppression, led to its permanent decline.

The Chartist Land Company attempted to give workers another means of subsistence by owning land. Its official registration (with lists of shareholders) is at TNA (BT 41/474/2659, BT 41/475/2659 and BT 41/476/2659).

Mark Crail's Chartist Ancestors website has a comprehensive overview of the movement, www.chartists.net. There's a list of Manchester Chartists, http://bit.ly/1RWmhpG, and over 300 Salford Chartists who subscribed to the Land Plan, http://bit.ly/24wx80L. The website also has a Chartist Ancestors Databank, www.chartists.net/chartist-ancestors-databank/.

See Malcolm Chase, *Chartism: A New History* (Manchester University Press, 2007) and J.F.C. Harrison and Dorothy Thompson, *Bibliography of the Chartist movement 1837–1976* (Harvester Press, 1978). For local detail, see Edmund and Ruth Frow, *Manchester and Salford Chartists* (Lancashire Community Press, 1996) and *Chartism in Manchester 1838–58* (Manchester Free Press, 1980) by the same authors.

The MLFHS website has a free surname and subject index to Edmund and Ruth Frow, *Radical Salford: Episodes In Labour History* (Neil Richardson, 1984), www.mlfhs.org.uk/data/4052.pdf. The Working Class Movement Library has a considerable collection of Chartism materials, including the *Northern Star* on microfilm, www.wcml.org.uk/our-collections/protest-politics-and-campaigning-for-change/chartist-movement/.

Votes For Women!

Although some thinkers such as John Stuart Mill had called for women to have equal voting rights with men, it was not until the late 1860s that pressure really began building for reform. Manchester's Free Trade Hall was the venue for the first meeting on women's suffrage in 1868, and Lancashire-born writer Lydia Ernestine Becker was one of the speakers.

The following year, the Municipal Corporations Amendment Act of 1869 enabled women (with a property qualification) to vote in local government elections and act as Poor Law Guardians. Emmeline Pankhurst was elected a member of the Chorlton Board of Guardians in 1895.

The National Union of Women's Suffrage Societies (1897) advocated peaceful constitutional reform. However, when peaceful efforts to give women the franchise failed repeatedly, members of the movement such as the Pankhurst family became increasingly militant. The Women's Social and Political Union (1903), led by Emmeline Pankhurst, switched to direct action. For example, in 1913 several suffragettes broke the glass of thirteen pictures at Manchester City Art Gallery.

Many suffragettes went to prison for their beliefs, and some went on hunger strike, and endured the horrors of artificial force-feeding. In August 1914, the Home Office compiled an index of the names of over 1,300 suffragettes who had been arrested, along with the number of times arrested and the locations (TNA, HO 45/24665). Ancestry has digitized this index; the collection, 1906–14 includes over 100 male campaigners.

At last the Representation of the People Act (1918) enfranchised women for the first time, but they had to be at least 30 years old, and there was a property qualification. When all women over age 21 were given the vote in 1928, they finally had an equal franchise with men.

The Women's Suffrage collections at MCL(M) are available on microfilm (cabinet 28); MCL has a guide. The collections include the Manchester Society for Women's Suffrage, 1867–1919 including annual reports and newspaper cuttings (M50/1). The society went through several name changes. Lydia Becker was the society's secretary, and her letter book for March–November 1868 has survived (M50/1/3).

These collections also include the papers of Millicent Garrett Fawcett, former President of the National Union of Women's Suffrage Societies (M50/2–8). Photos and memorabilia of members of the Women's Social and Political Union are in series MISC/504. Many men and women were opposed to women's suffrage, and MCL(M) also holds papers for the Manchester branch of the National League for Opposing Women's Suffrage (M131).

The JRL has four important collections: the Parliamentary Committee for Women's Suffrage, 1892–1903; Manchester Men's League for Women's Suffrage, 1909–18; National Union of Women's Suffrage Societies, 1910–14; and the International Woman Suffrage Alliance, 1913–20, http://bit.ly/1P4Vyr0.

See Emmeline Pankhurst, *My Own Story* (London, 1914); Michael Herbert, *Up Then Brave Women: Manchester's Radical Women 1819–1918* (North West Labour History Society, n.d.); Elizabeth Crawford, *The Women's Suffrage Movement: A Reference Guide 1866–1928* (Routledge, 2001); and Elizabeth Crawford, *The Women's Suffrage Movement in Britain and Ireland: a regional survey* (Routledge, 2001).

Emmeline Pankhurst's home at 62 Nelson Street, Manchester is now a museum and heritage centre, www.thepankhurstcentre.org.uk/.

ELECTORAL REGISTERS

After the 1832 Reform Act, Manchester was granted two MPs, and Salford had one. However, in boroughs the vote was restricted to men with property worth £10 p.a. For county elections, some copyholders, leaseholders and tenants were enfranchised in addition to 40s. freeholders. The news that Manchester was enfranchised at last was celebrated with a magnificent procession through the streets, and Mr Charles Green made a balloon ascent. Later that year, the Liberals Mark Philips and Charles Poulett-Thompson were elected for Manchester, and the Radical Joseph Brotherton for Salford.

The franchise for men was only broadened gradually. In 1867 male householders in towns, lodgers paying £10 or more in rent and some smallholders in rural areas were given the vote. The franchise was extended to all male householders in the town and country. However, many poor working class men still could not vote. It was not until 1918 that all men over the age of 21 were given the vote.

Electoral registers are arranged by street, so you need a good idea of where your ancestor was living before you consult them. They do not have a surname index. MLFHS has an online guide, http://mlfhs. org.uk/guides/researching_electoral_registers.pdf.

The Manchester borough-reeve's records at MCL(M) include the borough register of electors, 1832–9 available on microfilm (M91). MCL has City of Manchester electoral registers, 1832–1993 on microfilm (but not 1917, 1940–4); there's an online guide, http://bit.ly/2hmyv0V.

Findmypast's Manchester collection of electoral registers, 1832–1900 covers Ardwick, Bradford, Beswick, Cheetham, Chorlton-upon-Medlock, Harpurhey, Hulme, Newton, Salford, Broughton and Manchester.

The township records for Salford at SCA include lists of electors; SLHL has copies of electoral registers for Salford, Eccles, Swinton, Pendlebury and Worsley.

TRADE UNIONS AND THE LABOUR MOVEMENT

Trade unions or 'combinations' of workers were banned until the late 1820s. Trade unions were natural successors to friendly societies. Funeral benefits were paid upon the death of a spouse, and many unions paid a pension to members too old or infirm to work.

The nineteenth century was punctuated by a series of strikes and trade disputes. John Doherty, the secretary of the Manchester spinners'

Statue of Joseph Brotherton (1753–1857), MP for Salford for over two decades.
Brotherton was the first person buried in Weaste Cemetery. (© Sue Wilkes)

union, was an early proponent of trade unions banding together to protect themselves against exploitation. However, his Grand Union of Cotton Operatives (1828) proved short-lived.

In the early 1860s skilled brick-makers reacted to the introduction of new machinery with violence. The Manchester and Salford Trades Council was formed in 1866 to coordinate peaceful resolutions to disputes. Two years later the Council hosted a Congress of trade councils and federations of trade societies, held at the Mechanics' Institution in Manchester. Some delegates from local trade unions attended. The Congress later became the Trades Union Congress (TUC). See Sidney and B.P. Webb and R.A. Peddie, *History of Trade Unionism* (BiblioLife, 2009) and A.E. Musson, *Trade Union and Social History* (Routledge, 1974).

MLIA holds records for several trade unions; search GMLives for more details. The Modern Records Centre, University of Warwick (see below) holds the largest collection of trade-union records; several of its union membership registers are available on Findmypast.

After all working class men gained the vote, the time was ripe for the formation of the Labour Party. Many books have been written on the party's history. See for example, Henry Pelling, *A Short History of the Labour Party* (7th edn) (Macmillan, 1982); Martin Pugh, *Speak for Britain!* (Vintage Books, 2011); and D. McHugh, *Labour in the City: The Development of the Labour Party in Manchester 1918–1931* (Manchester University Press, 2007).

Labour, Working Class and Political Archives
LABOUR HISTORY ARCHIVE AND LOCAL STUDY CENTRE, MANCHESTER
The People's History Museum is home to the archives of working class organizations from the Chartists to New Labour, including the Labour Party and the Communist Party of Great Britain, with personal papers of politicians, writers, activists and more. Visits to the archive are by appointment. The website has guides to its collections on the British Union of Fascists, early industrial Manchester, the 1984–5 miners' strike, general elections, Spanish Civil War, Chartism and women's suffrage, www.phm.org.uk/archive-study-centre/online-catalogue/.

MODERN RECORDS CENTRE, UNIVERSITY OF WARWICK
The centre holds records for employers' associations, trade associations

and trade unions for different industries. Union records do not necessarily include membership registers. The centre also holds the Trades Union Congress archive, and Transport and General Workers Union archive. Readers should contact the Centre before visiting to check availability, www2.warwick.ac.uk/services/library/mrc/holdings/main_archives.

WORKING CLASS MOVEMENT LIBRARY

The Working Class Movement Library in Salford has comprehensive collections of books, pamphlets, journals, banners and ephemera on people's working lives, trade unions, the Labour Party, Radicals, Chartists and the co-operative movement, www.wcml.org.uk. Trades covered include boiler makers, gas workers, miners, railway workers, etc. Typical trade-union records include annual reports, branch records, minute books, membership cards, members' lists, sickness and benefit books, etc. The library also has resources for Black and Asian history, e.g., the Pan-African Congress held in Manchester in 1945. Oral histories include the memories of miners who worked at Agecroft Colliery in Salford, https://invisiblehistoriesproject.wordpress.com/work places/agecroft-colliery/.

Working Class Movement Library, Salford. (© Sue Wilkes)

CO-OPERATIVE SOCIETIES

Unlike trade unions, co-operative societies were not frowned on by the authorities as they were believed to encourage thrift. The movement was inspired by Robert Owen's ideals. The first Co-operative Congress was held in Manchester in 1833, and the Co-operative Wholesale Society was formed in the city three decades later. MCL(M) holds records for the Manchester and Salford Equitable Co-operative Society, 1859–1982 (M437).

National Co-operative Archive, Manchester

The archive holds original records for national co-operative organizations and societies: periodicals, books, pamphlets, photographs, personal papers and letters. The Co-operative Women's Guild (Lancashire Region) collection includes Manchester and Salford District records for 1911–2008: minute books, cash books, attendance records, press cuttings and photos (LCWG/1). It also holds the National Co-operative Film Archive and records for the Co-operative Wholesale Society, www.archive.coop and www.archive.coop/collections/coop-wholesale-society.

THE ANTI-CORN LAW MOVEMENT

The Corn Laws were first introduced in 1815 to protect the land-owning classes. In effect, the legislation kept the price of bread artificially high. These laws were greatly resented by the workers, and hand-loom weavers petitioned Parliament for their repeal. Manufacturers like Richard Cobden and John Bright, however, saw the Corn Laws as an interference with free trade. They felt they could not lower their workers' wages, either, while bread was so expensive. The first meeting of an Anti-Corn Law Association was in London in 1836; Archibald Prentice, a Manchester Radical, was on the committee.

An Anti-Corn Law Association was formed in Manchester on 24 September 1838 at the York Hotel in King Street. The association, later renamed the Anti-Corn Law League, spread far and wide. It was primarily a middle-class movement. The league lobbied Parliament and printed circulars in favour of reform. When Sir Robert Peel repealed the Corn Laws in 1846, a general holiday was declared in Manchester; there was a grand procession on 3 August, and the city was illuminated.

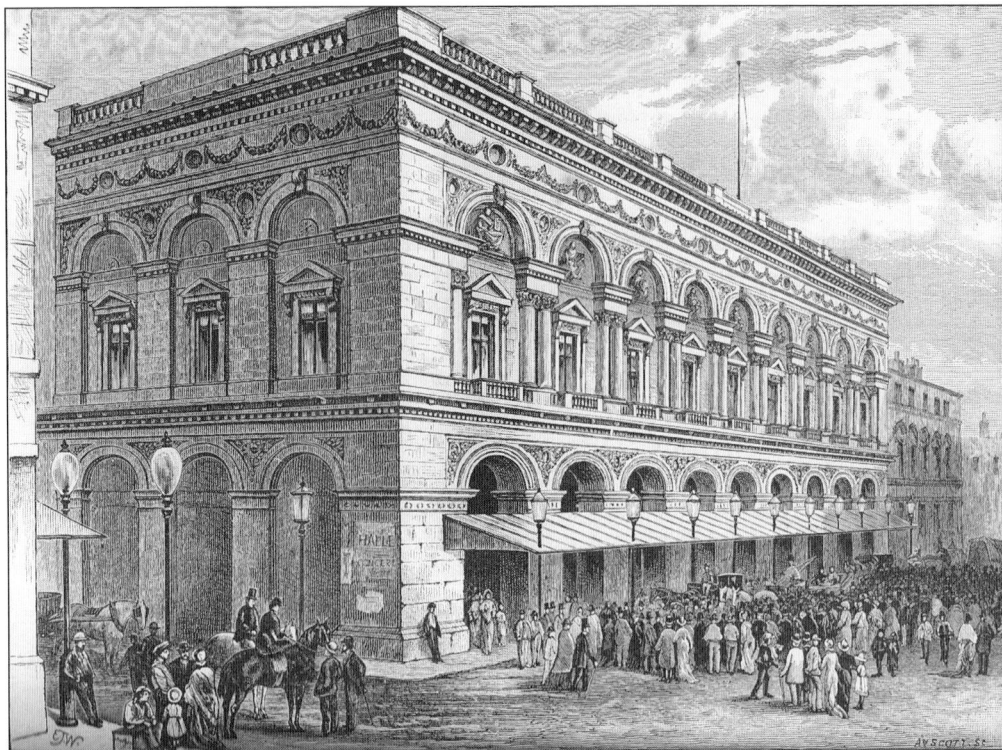

Free Trade Hall, Manchester, built in the 1850s to commemorate the repeal of the Corn Laws. Our Own Country *(Cassell & Co., n.d., c.1883), Vol. III. (Author's collection)*

See Paul Pickering and Alex Tyrell, *The People's Bread: A History of the Anti-Corn Law League* (Leicester University Press, 2000) and Archibald Prentice, *History of the Anti-Corn Law League*, 2 vols (1853).

MCL(M) holds the papers of George Wilson, league chairman, with over 5,000 items of correspondence (M20/1–41). An index is available. It also holds a collection of Richard Cobden's correspondence (M87).

MIGRATION EXPERIENCES

The court leet records and constables' accounts may contain some of the earliest records of Scottish and Irish migrants and people from far-flung Europe arriving and living in Manchester and Salford.

During the Industrial Revolution, both towns witnessed an unprecedented increase in population. According to John Aikin, a survey of the local population in 1773 found that Manchester had 3,402 inhabited houses, accommodating 5,317 families (22,481 people).

Salford had 866 inhabited houses with 1,099 families (4,765 people).

By 1801, Manchester township contained 70,409 people and Salford township had 13,611 people. Within 2 decades, Manchester had over 108,000 souls, and Salford's population had almost doubled to 25,772 people.

The reasons for this massive population growth are complex, but primarily the rise of the cotton industry and dependent trades, and the transport revolution, attracted entrepreneurs as well as thousands of migrants looking for work. Plenty of jobs were available for children and young persons, too, which made people more likely to marry at an early age and have lots of offspring.

Many immigrants made a significant contribution to the area's civic life, commerce, industry and scientific achievements. For example, engineer James Nasmyth was a Scot, as were factory owners James McConnel and John Kennedy (papers at JRL: MCK). Louis Schwabe, a silk manufacturer who married into an old Manchester family, was a German Jew. Dr Louis Borchadt, also from Germany, worked at Manchester's Children's Dispensary. The suburb of Greenheys was home to several German families.

The Irish

Manchester's Irish communities took root during the late eighteenth and early nineteenth centuries. Their numbers were swelled by families fleeing the potato famine of the 1840s, and by 1851 over 13 per cent of the city's population was Irish – its largest ethnic community. The Irish took unskilled work such as labouring or navvying, or learned hand-loom weaving – an industry in long-term decline. They endured some of the worst housing conditions in Manchester as their wages were so low.

For graphic descriptions of the poorest districts, including the infamous 'Little Ireland', see Friedrich Engels, *The Condition of the Working Class in England* (Oxford University Press, 1993) and James P. Kay-Shuttleworth, *The Moral and Physical Condition of the Working Classes Employed in the Cotton Manufacture in Manchester (1832)* (2nd edn) (Frank Cass & Co. Ltd, 1970).

However, for a modern assessment of Engels and Kay-Shuttleworth's reportage of Irish communities, see Mervyn Busteed, *The Irish in Manchester c.1750–1921* (Manchester University Press, 2016). See also Mervyn Busteed, Robert I. Hodgson and Thomas F. Kennedy,

The myth and reality of Irish migrants in mid-19th century Manchester (Leicester University Press, 1992) and Roger Swift, *Irish Migrants in Britain, 1815–1914* (Cork University Press, 2002).

MLIA has online guides to its collections for communities from other parts of the UK, as follows:

• The Irish community, www.manchester.gov.uk/directory record/ 212561/irish
• The Scottish community, www.manchester.gov.uk/directory record/ 212567/scottish
• The Welsh community, www.manchester.gov.uk/directory record/ 212570/welsh

The Jewish Community

Jews may have visited the Manchester area as early as the 1740s. Travelling chapmen seemingly faced some prejudice by locals worried that they would steal the secrets of the town's burgeoning textile industries. By the 1790s, several tradesmen were living in Manchester's Old Town (the Shudehill district) and in the early 1800s there was a small synagogue in Garden Street, Withy Grove. A few years later it moved to Ainsworth's Court, Long Millgate. A new synagogue was erected on Halliwell Street, Long Millgate, in 1825; its first minister was the Revd Abraham Abrahams. There was also a Jewish burial ground near St Thomas' chapel in Pendleton, Salford.

Around this time, Nathan Meyer Rothschild, of the famous banking family, settled in Manchester. He became a British citizen, and lived in a smart residence in Ardwick, before moving to London to further his banking career. The Behrens family, too, became successful merchants, and they had elegant homes in Higher Broughton and Plymouth Grove.

During Victoria's reign, persecution in Europe and Russia led to the arrival of large numbers of Jews. Two Jewish synagogues were in use on Cheetham Hill Road by the late 1850s, and the community had schools on York Street. See Bill Williams, *The Making of Manchester Jewry 1740–1875* (Manchester University Press, 1985).

In the Second World War millions of refugees, both Jews and non-Jews, fled Nazi-occupied Europe and several thousand arrived in Manchester. For the work done by local refugee committees of all denominations, see Bill Williams, *Jews and Other Foreigners: Manchester and the Rescue of Victims of European Fascism 1933–40* (Manchester University Press, 2011).

MCL(M) has several collections relating to the Jewish community including burial registers, school admission registers and Manchester Great Synagogue membership records. There's an online guide, http://www.manchester.gov.uk/directoryrecord/212563/jewish.

The archive's collections include historian Bill Williams' research papers (M790). For Second World War refugees, see the Manchester Jewish Refugees Committee records (M102, M112, and M533 (some restricted access)). The M533 series includes papers for the Council of Manchester and Salford Jews, 1945–7, and Manchester and Salford Council of Social Services, 1943–52.

The Manchester Naturalization Society was a scheme by which members could afford naturalization papers. Members paid a weekly fee, and a ballot was held; the lucky winners were given funds to apply for British citizenship. MCL(M) has a cash book, 1896–1909 (M150), with over 500 names; an index is available on Findmypast.

The records of the Manchester Jewish Working Men's Club at MCL(G) include minute books for 1926–35 and 1941–62 with members' names; the earlier book includes some members' addresses (M154). MCL has copies of the *Jewish Chronicle* on microfilm (a day's notice is required to view it).

• The Manchester Jewry Database was compiled from city directories for 1855, 1888, 1927 and 1934; www.jewishgen.org/jcr-uk/Community/man_street.htm.
• The Manchester Jewish Community home page has a list of synagogues in Greater Manchester (with weblinks): www.jewishgen.org/jcr-uk/Manchester.htm.

Manchester Jewish Museum
The museum, housed in the oldest surviving synagogue in Manchester, tells the story of the area's Jewish population. The Jewish Genealogical Society of Great Britain holds meetings here, www.manchesterjewish museum.com.

Sources for Migrants and Foreign Residents
Historical trade directories, the censuses and newspapers are good

sources for foreign names. Churchwardens' and Poor Law records are particularly useful for the impoverished Irish community. If you are looking for an ancestor who left Manchester and Salford for a new life abroad, TNA's Outward Passenger Lists collection (BT 27) for long-distance voyages leaving Britain, 1890–1960 is available on Findmypast.

John Scholes' 'Lists of Foreign Merchants in Manchester 1784–1870' is available at MCL on microfilm (MF1286), and digitized images are on Flickr, http://bit.ly/1UauDeI. The Scholes lists are a good source for the Greek community.

It is beyond the scope of this work to give a full list of sources for such a culturally diverse region. Some resources for African, African Caribbean, Armenian, Asian, Chinese and Polish migrants are listed in the Further Reading section at the end of this chapter. If researching the Muslim community, search GMLives for photos and other records of mosques, youth clubs, etc.

MLIA has online guides to sources for several ethnic groups, including the following:

- African community, http://bit.ly/2hPvaZp.
- African-Caribbean community, http://bit.ly/2i5inFs.
- Early Arab and Muslim communities, http://bit.ly/2hDPDm6.
- Armenian community, http://bit.ly/2hQhpfJ.
- Belarussian community, http://bit.ly/2gXD7cS.
- Belgian refugees, http://bit.ly/2h6dNVp.
- Chinese community, http://bit.ly/2h6dY31.
- German community, http://bit.ly/2hQqrcx.
- Hungarian community, http://bit.ly/2hmGxql.
- Italian community, http://bit.ly/2hmDpv1.
- Kosovans and other refugee groups in the 1990s/2000s, http://bit.ly/2i5dprY.
- Polish community, http://bit.ly/2hDK6vD.
- South Asian communities, http://bit.ly/2h5X6cl.
- Ukrainian community, http://bit.ly/2hDIORA.

AHMED IQBAL ULLAH RACE RELATIONS RESOURCE CENTRE, UNIVERSITY OF MANCHESTER (AT MCL)

The centre, on the lower ground floor of MCL, has a race and ethnic history library with an important oral history collection. Collections include the library of the Commission for Racial Equality, and Steve Cohen's collection of memorabilia from anti-deportation and immigration campaigns in Manchester from the 1970s–90s. MCL library members can borrow books from the centre's library, www.race archive.manchester.ac.uk.

THE MANCHESTER CHINESE ARCHIVE

This archive is the result of a community project created with the help of local archives and museums. The website discusses the problems facing people researching their Chinese ancestors in the Greater Manchester area. There are useful pages on census entries, Chinese genealogy and archives, and businesses. The archive at MCL(M) includes oral histories, personal papers and photos (the documents are mostly written in Chinese) (CHI). www.manchesterchinesearchive. org.uk.

WARTIME EXPERIENCES
Militia and Volunteer Regiments

Some of the earliest Manchester regiments were formed during the English Civil War. Manchester was on the side of the Parliamentarians, and Sir Thomas Fairfax made the town his headquarters; Salford backed the Royalists. Two regiments underwent 'foreign' service at Wigan, where they were defeated by the Royalists in late 1642. However, on Christmas Eve the Manchester regiments won the Battle of Chowbent and defeated the Royalists.

When the Civil War broke out, adult males were asked to take an oath of allegiance. See 'The Protestation of 1641–2 in Manchester', *Palatine Notebook 1*, 1881; 'The Manchester Protestation of 1641–1642', Vol. 30, Pts 1 and 2, *MG*, 1994; and 'The Protestators of Salford . . . 1641–1642', *Palatine Notebook 4*, 1884.

Royalist Composition Papers (TNA, SP 23) list the fines paid by Royalists for their part in the war after the defeat of Charles I. The Composition Papers for Lancashire have been published by the LCRS. After the Restoration, people were also asked to take an oath of allegiance. See John Harland, 'The names of eight hundred inhabitants of Manchester who took the oath of allegiance to Charles II in April 1679', *Chetham Miscellanies 3*, CS, Vol. 57, 1862.

Another 'Manchester Regiment' was formed during the Jacobite rebellion of 1745, when Prince Charles Edward Stuart and his rebel army marched through Manchester and Salford. Colonel Francis Towneley and a couple of hundred Manchester men went south with 'Bonnie Prince Charlie'. After the prince's defeat at Culloden, Towneley and several other officers were found guilty of treason and executed at London. The heads of two Manchester rebels were brought to the town and placed on display at the Exchange; this horrible sight caused much ill-feeling locally.

Many volunteer and militia regiments sprang up during the eighteenth and nineteenth centuries, some as a response to the threat of invasion. The Manchester and Salford Volunteers, commanded by Colonel T.B. Bayley, were formed in 1799. After the short-lived Peace of Amiens, in 1803 several volunteer corps were formed at Manchester, Pendleton, Hulme and Trafford. The LA website has a guide to sources for Lancashire militia and volunteer regiments after 1757, www. lancashire.gov.uk/media/52092/Handlist72militiaandvolunteers.pdf.

MCL(G)'s collection for the Egerton family of Heaton Hall includes militia papers of the Royal Manchester Volunteers (72nd Regiment), 1782–8, and the Royal Lancashire Volunteers, 1779–94, including a register of recruits, a muster roll, courts martial and volunteers' certificates (E4).

There's an online database of the Royal Lancashire Volunteer Regiment's register of recruits, 1779–82, which includes Manchester and Salford men. Each man's name, occupation, place of origin and physical details are listed. The 'remarks' section sometimes includes date of death or date discharged: www.manchester.gov.uk/downloads/ download/4205/royal_lancashire_regiment.

Findmypast's Militia Attestations Index (TNA, WO96), 1860–1915 includes Lancashire regiments (attestations are forms with recruits' personal details). See Jeremy Gibson and Mervyn Medlycott, *Militia Lists and Musters 1757–1876: A Directory of Holdings in the British Isles* (5th edn) (Family History Partnership, 2013).

First World War
Shortly after the outbreak of the First World War, thousands of Manchester and Salford men answered the call to arms. Some were already serving in the Territorial Army (42nd East Lancashire Division). This division included the Lancashire Fusiliers, which had two

battalions based at Cross Lane barracks in Salford, and the Manchester Infantry Brigade: 5th, 6th, 7th and 8th Battalions. The 'Terriers', as they were nicknamed, were initially sent to Egypt.

A recruitment drive began in earnest in the summer of 1914. The Manchester Regiment was formed in 1881 from the 63rd and 96th Regiments of Foot; it had witnessed many campaigns abroad in defence of the Empire. The regiment raised three service battalions (11th, 12th and 13th), but again, some new recruits were posted to distant regiments.

Then in late August the 'Pals' movement began; men were assured that if they joined up, they could serve with their friends. The regiment raised eight service battalions (16th–23rd) in Manchester city, including a 'bantam' battalion (for men below the 5ft 3in height limit), as well as another battalion in Oldham (24th). In Salford, four 'Pals' battalions were raised: the 15th, 16th, 19th and 20th Battalions of the Lancashire Fusiliers.

Civilians also 'did their bit'. Women worked on the trams and buses and as lorry drivers. Food rationing was introduced. School buildings in Manchester and Salford were used as military hospitals, and girl guides worked as hospital orderlies. Thousands of pounds were raised for the war effort, homes for disabled servicemen, local charities and refugees. Over 3,000 Belgians arrived in the Manchester area, and SCA holds minutes for the Belgian Refugee Committee, 1914–15 (U8).

The North West Film Archive has published a DVD, *The First World War: Life On the Home Front in North-West England*, which is available from MCL and several local museums, http://bit.ly/24k31JT. There's a trailer online, http://bit.ly/1XjoDrh.

Local and national newspapers reported the sickening toll of deaths, missing soldiers and injuries each week as millions of men fought and died on the battlefields of France, Belgium and other far-flung places. Local papers often published photos of servicemen.

Not everyone in Manchester and Salford gave their unqualified support to the war. Conscientious Objectors refused to serve, and some socialists and pacifists were opposed to the bloodshed. See Alison Ronan, *Unpopular Resistance* (North West Labour History Society, n.d.).

First World War Resources

Readers should not assume that a local ancestor served in the

Manchester or Salford 'Pals'; Manchester and Salford men also served in the East Lancashire Regiment and other units. Some genealogy guides on military sources are listed in the Further Reading section at the end of this chapter.

Several online genealogy suppliers offer First World War and Second World War death indexes, rolls of honour and copies of 'Soldiers Died in the Great War'. Findmypast's collections include the rolls of honour for the Salford Pals, Manchester employers and an index to the Manchester Regiment's City Battalions Book of Honour. Ancestry's collections include British Army WW1 Service Records and Pension Records, 1914–20, and Service Medals and Awards.

Many books have been published on the world wars, battlefields and individual regiments; only a brief survey can be given here. See Terry Wyke and Nigel Rudyard, *Military History in the North West* (Manchester: Bibliography of North West England, 1994).

See also, for example, Frederick Gibbon, *The 42nd (East Lancashire Division) 1914–18* (repr. Naval and Military Press, 2015); Michael Stedman, *Manchester Pals* (repr. Pen & Sword Military, 2014); John Hartley, *6th Battalion: The Manchester Regiment in the Great War* (Pen & Sword Military, 2010); Stephen Barker and Christopher Boardman, *Lancashire's Forgotten Heroes: 8th (Service) Battalion, East Lancashire Regiment in the Great War* (History Press, 2008); and Caroline Scott, *The Manchester Bantams* (Pen & Sword Military, 2016).

For Salford, see Michael Stedman, *Salford Pals* (Pen & Sword Military, 2007); Michael Stedman, *The Somme 1916: and other experiences of the Salford Pals* (Pen & Sword Military, 2006); and Neil Drum and Roger Dowson, *'God's Own': 1st Salford Pals* (Neil Richardson, 2003).

The Local Studies Library at MCL has copies of the *Manchester Regiment Gazette*, 1913–58 (356 M5) and several books on the history of the regiment. The Manchester Regiment's archive (for soldiers serving before 1958, when it merged with the King's Regiment) is at Tameside Local Studies and Archives, www.tameside.gov.uk/archives/manchesterregiment.

There's an online images archive (search by battalion or keyword) www.manchester-regiment.org.uk/about.php. Ashton Town Hall has a museum dedicated to the Manchesters.

The regimental archive for the Queen's Lancashire Regiment and its predecessors, the Loyal North Lancashire Regiment (Prince of

Wales's Volunteers), East Lancashire Regment, South Lancashire Regiment, the 30th, 40th, 47th, 59th, 81st and 82nd Regiments of Foot, and the Royal Lancashire Militia, is at the Lancashire Infantry Museum, Preston, www.lancashireinfantrymuseum.org.uk/research/. The archive at the museum is open to visitors by appointment only. A research service (fee payable) is available.

Salford Museum and Art Gallery has several local rolls of honour in display, including the 16th Lancashire Fusiliers Roll for Swinton and Pendlebury, www.salfordwarmemorials.co.uk/16th-lancashire-fusiliers-e-company.html.

• The Lancashire Online Parish Clerks website has an index to Salford's 'Absent Voters' (men on service), www.lan-opc.org.uk/Salford/Electors/index.html.
• Lancashire Archives has an online guide to its First World War collections, www.lancashire.gov.uk/media/166101/Handlist-WW1-Lancashire-Archives-24-May-2013.pdf.
• TNA's website has dozens of guides on how to find records for the First World War and Second World War including military, nursing, RAF, maritime, POWs, etc., www.nationalarchives.gov.uk/help-with-your-research/#find-a-research-guide. TNA is currently digitizing the regimental war diaries for the First World War, http://bit.ly/1GHDrSz.
• The Commonwealth War Graves Commission has a free 'Debt of Honour Register' database for casualties, including commonwealth citizens, who died in the First World War or Second World War. There's a searchable database of cemeteries. Sometimes casualty details include the name and address of next of kin, www.cwgc.org/.

MANCHESTER WAR MEMORIALS
MLFHS is currently compiling a free index to Manchester war memorials (First World War and Second World War). At the time of writing, over 42,000 names have been indexed. The list of memorials has photos of most of the memorials, and links to the War Memorials Register; Salford and Eccles monuments are included. You can search the index of names, and index of memorials at www.mlfhs.org.uk/data/war_memorials.php. See Stephen Lowe, *List of war memorials within the City of Manchester* (S. Lowe, 2001).

Salford War Memorials

The website includes the 1918 Absent Voters' List for Salford; the Manchester & Salford Roll of Honour; *Eccles Journal* Roll of Honour with index; *Manchester Evening News* First World War Index; Adelphi Lads' Club Roll of Honour; *Salford Reporter* First World War Index; *Eccles Journal* First World War Index; and the Parish of St Thomas, Pendleton, Roll of Honour, www.salfordwarmemorials.co.uk/resources.html#AVL.

National Registration in the First World War

On 15 August 1915, all persons aged 15–65 registered their name, age, address, marital status, number of dependents, nationality (for non-British) and employment details. People serving in the armed forces, or living in workhouses, hospitals (including mental institutions) and prisons, were exempt from registration. The registers were updated when persons changed address. A few national registration cards, certificates and ration books from both world wars may be held locally.

Second World War
The 1939 Register

A similar scheme was also in force during the Second World War. On 29 September 1939 every man, woman and child in England and Wales was recorded and given a national registration number, except for armed forces members serving away from home and merchant seamen. Each person was given an identity (ID) card. People needed their ID card in order to obtain a ration book; there was a charge for lost cards. The register was updated when people moved house or changed their marital status.

After 1952, however, people no longer had to carry ID cards and the system ceased. National registration numbers were used as National Health Service numbers when the scheme was introduced in 1948. TNA has a guide to the register, www.nationalarchives.gov.uk/help-with-your-research/research-guides/1939-register.

The 1939 Register has been digitized by Findmypast in partnership with TNA, www.findmypast.co.uk/1939register; it's free to search by surname and location. Images of the register are free to subscribers and can be viewed free in TNA reading rooms, and also on MCC library computers. Records of people younger than 100 years who are still alive, or who died after 1991, are redacted on the register.

THE BLITZ AND EVACUEES

The Manchester area was lucky in one respect during the First World War. It suffered very few Zeppelin raids, although some Bolton people were killed in September 1916. However, in the Second World War Manchester and Salford were prime targets for German bombers because they were important industrial centres.

Some of Manchester's most historic buildings suffered in the terrifying 'Christmas Blitz' of 22 and 23 December 1940. The city's much loved Cathedral, Royal Exchange, Free Trade Hall, Chetham's Hospital, Assize Courts, Trafford Hall and Trafford Park were badly damaged. The impact on families was horrifying, too: hundreds of people were killed and thousands wounded. Many people lost their homes. Over 1,400 Second World War civilian dead are listed, with details of their death if known, on the Greater Manchester Blitz Victims website, www.greater manchesterblitzvictims.co.uk/.

It can be difficult researching wartime events because the press was censored. Only limited coverage of bombings was permitted, and the censor kept a weather eye on any editorial comment in the newspapers. See Guy Hodgson, *War Torn: Manchester, Its Newspapers, and the Luftwaffe's Christmas Blitz of 1940* (University of Chester Press, 2015).

The Blitz had been anticipated, and in September 1939 'Operation Pied Piper' began. Thousands of children, babies and expectant mothers were evacuated overseas and to the British countryside, away from the bombers. See John Welshman, *Churchill's Children, The Evacuee Experience in Wartime Britain* (Oxford University Press, 2010).

Evacuees' records are most likely to be in the archives of the reception authority – use TNA Discovery to locate them. Sensitive records may be closed for 100 years. LA has a list of unaccompanied children from Salford schools sent to Lancaster (DDX 2774/1). The same archive's Cyril Ainsworth Collection has a register of evacuees from several Manchester schools (DDX 1525), and the Fulwood school log book has a list of Manchester evacuees (SMFu/2). MCL(M)'s collection of school log books include evacuees. The Booth Hall Hospital admission registers also include evacuees (M302, Vol. 8).

Second World War Resources

MCL has an online guide to its Second World War collections, which include civil defence, air raids, Conscientious Objectors, evacuees,

Trafford Hall. The building was demolished shortly after it suffered bomb damage in the Second World War. Alfred Rimmer, Summer Rambles Around Manchester *(John Heywood, n.d., c.1890). (Author's collection)*

refugees, etc., http://bit.ly/2i5o45U. MLIA's photographic collections include hundreds of images relating to both world wars including memorials, soldiers, women workers, regiments and blitz damage (search GMLives and limit your search to 'photographs').

MCC published a *Book Of Remembrance* of civilian casualties; the Local Studies Reference Library has a copy. *Manchester Wartime Memories*, a book and audio CD-ROM published in 2005 by the City of Manchester to commemorate the sixtieth anniversary of the end of the Second World War, is available to buy from MCL. A selection of images from the book is on Flickr, http://bit.ly/1oUgn1n, and the original interviews recorded for the CD-ROM can be accessed via the search room (GMSA, BOX 290).

See also Graham Phythian, *Blitz Britain: Manchester and Salford* (History Press, 2015); C. Hardy, I. Cooper and H. Hochland, *Manchester at War* (Archive Productions Ltd, 1986); Donald Read, *A Manchester boyhood in the thirties and forties: growing up in war and peace* (Edwin Mellen Press, 2003); Simon Wright, *Memories of the Salford Blitz* (Neil Richardson, 1987); and Peter J.C. Smith, *Luftwaffe Over Manchester· The Blitz Years 1940–1944* (Neil Richardson, 2003). The MLFHS website has a free surname index of casualties (deceased and injured) mentioned in Peter Smith's book, www.mlfhs.org.uk/data/4511.pdf.

MCL(M) holds East Lancashire Territorial and Auxiliary Forces Association minutes, 1907–67 including records of formation, 1907–8, recruiting and discharge, 1908–12, 1919–22, 1936–40, 1947–67, and Home Guard papers (M73).

SCA holds a list of Swinton and Pendlebury borough civilian war deaths, 1940–1 and 1949, register of displaced persons, 1933–43, and papers relating to Air Raid Precautions personnel (LBSP). It also holds the 7th Eccles Home Guard Battalion minutes, cash book, etc.,1956–68 (U259); and Lancashire Home Guard accounts (U197; see also LA, HG).

The Liddle Collection at the University of Leeds comprises the personal papers (including artefacts, diaries and photos) of hundreds of people who lived through the world wars, including soldiers and civilians. Online indexes are available. https://library.leeds.ac.uk/special-collections-liddle-collection.

The UK government website has a guide to obtaining military service records after 1920, https://www.gov.uk/get-copy-military-service-records/overview.

A MESSAGE HOME: THE 'CALLING BLIGHTY' FILMS

If your ancestor served in the Far East during the Second World War, you can get a flavour of what life was like for them in the 'Calling Blighty' collection at the North West Film Archive. The films were made in India, Burma, Singapore and Malaya between 1944 and 1946, allowing service personnel to send a personal message home to family and friends, who were invited to a local cinema to see the film. More detailed information is available at www.nwfa.mmu.ac.uk/blighty/index.php. Of 391 films made, only around 50 survive in the UK's film archives, with half of these held at the NWFA – over 600 messages. A database of the name, rank and serial number of each person sending a message, their home town and the film clip is now searchable online at www.nwfa.mmu.ac.uk/blighty/search.php.

THE FIRE SERVICE

Manchester's surviving court leet records from the late seventeenth century mention a primitive fire engine. After 1828, fire prevention was under the supervision of the township Watch Committee. By 1839 the Manchester Police Fire Engine Establishment Department had seven fire engines and one horse (additional horses were hired when needed). The brigade's firemen received a new hat and uniform every two years.

An 1844 Act gave Manchester Corporation the power to form its own Fire Brigade, supervised by its own Watch Committee. During the late 1850s the Manchester Fire Brigade had a station in the police yard at Clarence Street. The brigade had 1 superintendent, 4 corporals, 8 branch men, 38 firemen and 10 fire engines. The firemen lived in cottages nearby. They were kept busy; in 1855 Manchester suffered 217 fires, of which 170 had to be extinguished using the engines.

The brigade moved to Jackson's Row, Albert Square, in 1865. By this date there were eleven fire stations in the city, including the Royal Infirmary and Assize Courts. The stations communicated by telegraph.

Salford and Pendleton had a fire brigade each and there was a voluntary force at Broughton, commanded by Captain Drew. The three forces merged in the early 1870s to form Salford Fire Brigade. See Robert F. Bonner, *Manchester Fire Brigade* (Archive Publications Ltd, 1988) and G.V. Blackstone, *A History of the British Fire Service* (Routledge & Kegan Paul, 1957).

During the Second World War a nationalized fire service was in operation. The National Fire Service was disbanded after the war, and control returned to local authorities. Manchester Fire Brigade became part of Greater Manchester Fire Service in 1974.

MCL(M) holds Manchester township Watch Committee records (M9). Manchester Fire Brigade records, 1830–1945, including fire record books, indexes of occupiers whose premises had suffered a fire, letter books, annual reports, lists of firemen, 1870–8, etc. are in series M1. The archive also has a call-out log book for all Manchester fire stations in 1949 (MISC/1216). MCL has a microfilm copy of notes made by a fire officer for a history of the brigade (MF444). MCL(G) holds records for the National Fire Service for the City of Salford area, 1941–8, including an incidence book and log books (GNFS).

SCA Services holds a fire register for Eccles Fire Brigade, 1916–42 and December 1945–February 1946 (LBE/7) and log books for Eccles Fire Station, 1949–56 (LLFE1).

Greater Manchester Fire Service Museum at Rochdale holds photos, cine film, video, audio tapes and printed material relating to the fire service. Researchers wishing to access the collections should contact the museum in advance, www.gmfsmuseum.org.uk/.

MODERN CITIES

After the Second World War, Manchester was faced with thousands of homes that were unfit for living in. New housing was built outside the city limits, and a programme of slum clearance began. By the 1980s unemployment was rife in inner city areas, which were also home to many immigrants including West Indian and Asian communities.

A new programme of regeneration began in Manchester and Salford in the late twentieth century. However, the 1996 IRA bomb caused great damage to Manchester city centre, including the Arndale shopping centre; mercifully, no one was killed. This gave developers and the council the opportunity to redevelop the city. Currently, many new buildings are planned, and the city's skyline is constantly changing. As well as museums and art galleries, the city centre has a thriving Chinatown and the Gay Village in Canal Street. MLIA has an online guide for its resources for the city's lesbian, gay, bisexual and transgender communities, http://bit.ly/2h5X1Ge.

In 1983 Salford City Council bought the old docks from the Ship Canal Company for redevelopment. The area, now known as 'Salford Quays', is home to MediaCity UK, the Lowry Centre and the Imperial War Museum North.

FURTHER READING

Begum, Rumana and Thompson, Andrew, *Asian 'Britishness', a study of first generation Asian migrants in Greater Manchester*, Institute for Public Policy Research, 2005

Bielewska, Agnieszka, *Changing Polish identities: post-war and post-accession Polish migrants in Manchester*, Peter Lang, 2012

Birchall, Johnston, *Co-op: The People's Business*, Manchester University Press, 1994

Bonner, Robert F., *Manchester Fire Brigade*, Archive Publications Ltd, 1988

Bullock, Roy, *Salford 1914–18: The County Borough and the First World War*, Neil Richardson, 2001

Christian, Peter, *Census: The Expert Guide*, TNA, 2008

Conway, Eddie, Frow, E. and R., Liddington, Jill, Luft, Mike, Norris, Jill, Rae, Tony, Thompson, Viv, *Labour History of Manchester and Salford: A Bibliography*, Manchester Centre for Marxist Education, 1978

Crail, Mark, *Tracing Your Labour Movement Ancestors*, Pen & Sword, 2009

Crawford, W.H., 'A Cosmopolitan City', in Frangopulo, N.J. (ed.), *Rich Inheritance: A Guide To The History Of Manchester*, Manchester Education Committee, 1961

Fowler, Simon, *Tracing Your First World War Ancestors*, Pen & Sword, 2013

George, Joan, *Merchants In Exile: The Armenians in Manchester, England, 1835–1935*, Gomidas Institute, 2002

Gibson, Jeremy and Medlycott, Mervyn, *Local census listings 1522–1930: Holdings in the British Isles*, 3rd edn, Federation of Family History Societies, 1997, repr. 2001

Grannum, Guy, *Tracing Your Caribbean Ancestors*, 3rd edn, A. & C. Black, 2013

Grenham, John, *Tracing Your Irish Ancestors*, 4th edn, Gill & Macmillan, 2012

Jeuda, Basil, *World War One and the Manchester Sephardim*, Shaare Hayim, 2014

Joseph, Anthony, *My Ancestors Were Jewish*, 4th edn, Society of Genealogists, 2008

Kershaw, Roger, *Migration Records: A Guide For Family Historians*, TNA, 2009

Lo, Sandy, *Chinese migrants: their experiences in their own words*, Manchester Metropolitan University, 2011

Maxwell, Ian, *Tracing Your Scottish Ancestors*, 2nd edn, Pen & Sword, 2014

Moody, David, *Scottish Family History*, Genealogical Publishing Company, 2010

Mounsey, W.H., *Migration in the Manchester area in recent pre-war years*, Manchester Statistical Society, 1941

Musson, A.E., *Trade Union and Social History*, Routledge, 2006

O'Neil, Joseph, *Manchester in the Great War*, Pen & Sword Military, 2014

Pickering, Paul, *Chartism and the Chartists in Manchester and Salford*, Macmillan, 1995

Prentice, Archibald, *Historical Sketches and Personal Recollections of Manchester*, 2nd edn, Manchester, 1851

Raymond, Stuart A., *Irish Family History On The Web*, 4th edn, Family History Partnership, 2015

Redford, Arthur, *Labour Migration in England 1800–1850*, Manchester University Press, 1976

Stanley, Jo, 'Mangoes to Moss Side: Caribbean Migration to Manchester in the 1950s and 1960s', *Manchester Region History Review*, Vol. 16, 2002–3; available online at http://bit.ly/24DFxCv

SuAndi, *Afro Solo UK: 39 life stories of African life in Greater Manchester 1920–1960*, artBlacklive 2014; available online at http://bit.ly/1sSYvXm

Tomaselli, Phil, *Tracing Your Second World War Ancestors*, Pen & Sword, 2011

Webb, Beatrice and Webb, Sidney, *History of Trade Unionism 1666–1920*, Webb and Webb, 1920

Wilkes, Sue, *Regency Cheshire*, Robert Hale, 2009

Wilkes, Sue, *Regency Spies*, Pen & Sword, 2015

Appendix 1

ARCHIVES AND RESOURCES

Ahmed Iqbal Ullah Race Relations Resource Centre, University of Manchester
Access to the collection is on the lower ground floor of MCL.
Postal enquiries: Ahmed Iqbal Ullah Race Relations Resource Centre, Central Library,
Manchester City Council, PO BOX 532, Albert Square, Manchester, M60 2LA
Website:www.racearchive.manchester.ac.uk
Email: rrarchive@manchester.ac.uk
Tel: 0161 275 2920

Archives+, MCL
Archives+ at MCL is a partnership between MLIA, GMCRO, MLFHS, Ahmed Iqbal Ullah Race Relations Resource Centre, North West Film Archive and the British Film Institute Mediatheque.
Each partner organization has its own separate website and online catalogue. See the separate listing in this section for each partner organization.
Website: www.archivesplus.org/more/catalogues/.

Barclays Group Archives, Manchester
Barclays Group Archives, Dallimore Road, Wythenshawe, Manchester, M23 9JA
Website: https://www.archive.barclays.com
Email: grouparchives@barclays.com
Tel: 0330 151 0159

Bolton Archives and Local Studies Services
Civic Centre, Le Mans Crescent, Bolton, BL1 1SE
Website: www.boltonlams.co.uk/archives

Email: archives@bolton.gov.uk
Tel: 0120 433 2185

Borthwick Institute for Archives

Cause Papers Database of cases heard 1300–1858 in diocese of York church courts: https://www.hrionline.ac.uk/causepapers; research guides and finding aids: www.york.ac.uk/borthwick/holdings/guides/. Borthwick Institute for Archives, University of York, Heslington, York, YO10 5DD
Website: www.york.ac.uk/borthwick
Email: borthwick-institute@york.ac.uk
Tel: 0190 432 1166

The British Library

Main catalogue: http://bit.ly/1Wg3Mk7; family history guide: www.bl. uk/familyhistory.html;
Manuscripts catalogue:
www.bl.uk/reshelp/findhelprestype/manuscripts/msscatalogues/mssc atalogues.html.
British Library, 96 Euston Road, London, NW1 2DB
Website: www.bl.uk
Email: customer-services@bl.uk
Tel: 0330 333 1144

The British Library, Boston Spa

National newspaper collection.
British Library, Boston Spa, Wetherby, West Yorkshire, LS23 7BQ
Website: www.bl.uk/reshelp/inrrooms/bspa/bostonspa.html
Email: customer-services@bl.uk
Tel: 0193 754 6060

Cheshire and Chester Archives and Local Studies

Catalogue search: http://archive.cheshire.gov.uk/calmview/.
Cheshire Archives and Local Studies Service, Cheshire Record Office, Duke Street, Chester, Cheshire, CH1 1RL
Website: http://archives.cheshire.gov.uk
Email: recordoffice@cheshiresharedservices.gov.uk
Tel: 0124 497 2574

Chetham's Library

The library's Flickr page includes old photos, slides and postcards of the Manchester area, photos of Belle Vue Gardens and over 700 images from the Mullineux collection; https://www.flickr.com/photos/chethams_library/; https://www.flickr.com/photos/chethams_library/albums; Digital Archive of Belle Vue Gardens. www.chethams.org.uk/bellevue/; Hand-list of Manuscripts: http://chethams.org.uk/wp-content/uploads/sites/3/2016/09/chethams_ manuscript_handlist.pdf; Library Catalogue: http://.chethams.org.uk/catalogue.html; Medieval manuscripts: http://chethams.org.uk/collections/archives-manuscripts/medieval-manuscripts/. Chetham's Library, Long Millgate, M3 1SB
Website: http://chethams.org.uk/
Email: librarian@chethams.org.uk
Tel: 0161 834 7961

Greater Manchester County Record Office at Manchester Central Library

See the MCL listing.

Greater Manchester Fire Service Museum

Collection of fire appliances and artefacts.
Maclure Road, Rochdale, OL11 1DN
Website: www.gmfsmuseum.org.uk
Email: museum@gmfsmuseum.org.uk
Tel: 0170 634 1219

Greater Manchester Police Museum and Archives

GMP Museum & Archives, 57a Newton Street, Manchester, M1 1ET
Website: www.gmpmuseum.co.uk/
Email: police.museum@gmp.police.uk
Tel: 0161 856 4500

Henry Watson Music Library

Rare manuscript collections and early printed music. See MCL listing.
Website: www.manchester.gov.uk/info/500138/central_library/6316/what_you_can_do_at_central_library/3
Email: henrywatsonmusiclibrary@manchester.gov.uk
Tel: 0161 234 1976

Labour History Archive and Local Study Centre, Manchester

Labour History Archive and Local Study Centre, People's History Museum, Left Bank, Spinningfields, Manchester, M3 3ER
Website: www.phm.org.uk/archive-study-centre
Email: archive@phm.org.uk
Tel: 0161 838 9190

Lancashire Archives

Church registers guide: www.lancashire.gov.uk/libraries-and-archives/archives-and-record-office/search-the-archives/church-registers-guide.aspx; research guides: www.lancashire.gov.uk/libraries-and-archives/archives-and-record-office/search-the-archives/research-guides.aspx
Lancashire Record Office, Bow Lane, Preston, Lancashire, PR1 2RE
Website: www.lancashire.gov.uk/libraries-and-archives/archives-and-record-office.aspx
Email: record.office@lancashire.gov.uk
Tel: 0177 253 3039

University of Leeds Special Collections

Special Collections, The Brotherton Library, University of Leeds, Leeds, LS2 9JT
Website:https://library.leeds.ac.uk/special-collections
Email: specialcollections@library.leeds.ac.uk
Tel: 0113 343 5518

Lichfield Record Office

Lichfield Record Office, The Friary, Lichfield, WS13 6QG
Website: www.staffordshire.gov.uk/leisure/archives/contact/Lichfield Record Office/home.aspx
Email: lichfield.record.office@staffordshire.gov.uk
Tel: 0154 351 0720

Liverpool Hope University Special Collections

Archives and Special Collections, The Sheppard-Worlock Library, Liverpool Hope University, Hope Park, Liverpool, L16 9JD
Website: www.hope.ac.uk/lifeathope/libraryandlearningspaces/special collections/
Email: specialcollections@hope.ac.uk
Tel: 0151 291 2027

Manchester Cathedral Archives

At least one week's notice is required to access items from the collections, which are produced for viewing at CL; contact Michael Powell, the Cathedral's Honorary Archivist, at Chetham's Library, Long Millgate, Manchester, M3 1SB.
Website: www.manchestercathedral.org/history/archives
Email (CL): librarian@chethams.org.uk
Tel: 0161 834 7961

Manchester Central Library

Home to GMCRO's and MCL(M)'s archives. Archival materials, rare books and special collections can be accessed in the search room; book an appointment before you visit. The reference collection is on the fourth floor. The first floor is home to the Henry Watson Music Library (see separate listing). Free wi-fi and public PCs are available throughout MCL. The historic Wolfson Reading Room is available for study purposes. MCL has disabled access.
Archives+ blog: https://manchesterarchiveplus. wordpress.com/
Archives+ website: www.archivesplus.org/
Archives+ Flickr page:
https://www.flickr.com/photos/manchesterarchiveplus/
Greater Manchester Lives Archives Catalogue:
http://gmlives.org.uk/index.html
Manchester Collection (Findmypast):
www.manchester.gov.uk/info/448/archives_and_local_history/5468/m anchester_collection
Library Catalogue: https://manchester.spydus.co.uk/
Rare books and special collections:
www.manchester.gov.uk/info/447/rare_books_and_special_collections
Manchester Central Library, St Peter's Square, Manchester, M2 5PD
Website, archives: www.manchester.gov.uk/info/448/archives_and_ local_history
Website, library: www.manchester.gov.uk/info/500138/ central_library
Email, archives: archiveslocalstudies@manchester.gov.uk
Email, library: libraries@manchester.gov.uk
Tel: archives: 0161 234 1979
Tel: library: 0161 234 1983

Manchester City Library
The library, home to the city's lending collection, is on the lower ground floor of MCL (the Town Hall extension basement). See the MCL listing for contact details.

Manchester City Council Libraries
Directory of Manchester City Libraries: www.manchester.gov.uk/directory/14/libraries

Manchester Grammar School Archive
Archive Catalogue: https://www.mgsarchives.org/archive-catalogue. Otto Smart, The Archivist, The Archive Room, Manchester Grammar School, Old Hall Lane, Manchester, M13 0XT
Website: https://www.mgsarchives.org
Email: archives@mgs.org
Tel: 0161 224 7201, ext. 361

Manchester High School for Girls Archive
Archive catalogue: www.mhsgarchive.org/catalogue.php.
Dr Christine A. Joy, School Archivist, Manchester High School for Girls, Grangethorpe Road, Rusholme, Manchester, M14 6HS
Website: www.mhsgarchive.org/
Email: cjoy@mhsg.manchester.sch.uk
Tel: 0161 249 2267

Manchester Jewish Museum
Researchers can access the museum's library and collections of documents, tapes and objects by prior appointment.
Manchester Jewish Museum, 190 Cheetham Hill Road, Manchester, M8 8LW
Website: www.manchesterjewishmuseum.com/
Email, curator: curator@manchesterjewishmuseum.com;
Email, general: admin@manchesterjewishmuseum.com
Tel, curator: 0161 830 1436
Tel, general: 0161 834 9879

Museum of Science and Industry, Manchester
The museum's Collections Centre has a study area and reference library.

Working mill engines, textile machinery demonstrations, transport history. Search the collections: http://emu.msim.org.uk/htmlmn/ collections /online/search.php.
Collections Department, Museum of Science and Industry, Liverpool Road, Castlefield, Manchester, M3 4FP
Website: http://msimanchester.org.uk/collection/research-and-study
Email: collections@msimanchester.org.uk
Tel, Collections Centre: 0161 606 0127
Tel, museum: 0161 832 2244

The National Archives
The National Archives, Kew, Richmond, Surrey, TW9 4DU
Website: www.nationalarchives.gov.uk
Email contact form: www.nationalarchives.gov.uk/contact/form
Tel: 0208 876 3444

National Co-operative Archive, Manchester
Visitors by appointment only. The archive's catalogues can be explored on the Archives Hub: http://archiveshub.ac.uk; Collections Overview: www.archive.coop/collections.
National Co-operative Archive, Holyoake House, Hanover Street, Manchester, M60 0AS
Website: www.archive.coop
Email: archive@co-op.ac.uk
Tel: 0161 819 3027/3028

National Gas Archive
Visitors by appointment only; a search fee is payable for all enquiries.
Unit 1, Europa Court, Europa Boulevard, Warrington, WA5 7TN
Website: www.gasarchive.org
Email: archive@nationalgrid.com
Tel: 0192 540 5130

North West Film Archive (NWFA)
Some material can be viewed online (identifiable in the online catalogue). There are also dedicated viewing Pods at Archives+ in MCL – free, and no appointment required. Researchers are welcome to visit by appointment to view other material, Mon–Fri, 9am–5pm. Online

Film and Video Catalogue available at: www.nwfa.mmu.ac.uk/default_
advsearch.htm; online catalogue of BBC Regional Holdings available
at: www.nwfa.mmu.ac.uk/bbc/default.htm; some excerpts from the
NWFA's collections are on Vimeo: https:// vimeo.com/nwfilmarchive.
North West Film Archive, Manchester Central Library, St Peter's Square,
Manchester, M2 5PD
Website: www.nwfa.mmu.ac.uk
Email n.w.filmarchive@mmu.ac.uk
Tel: 0161 247 3097

Oldham Local Studies & Archives

Local Studies & Archives, 84 Union Street, Oldham, OL1 1DN
Website: www.oldham.gov.uk/info/200390/family_history
Email: archives@oldham.gov.uk
Tel: 0161 770 4654

Portico Library

Subscription library. Membership fee; restricted number of members.
Gallery open to general public. Researchers are welcome to consult the
library's collection (membership not required), but only members are
permitted to borrow books.
57 Mosley Street, Manchester, M2 3FF
Website: www.theportico.org.uk
Email: librarian@theportico.org.uk
Tel: 0161 236 6785

Royal Bank of Scotland Archives

RBS Archives, 6 South Gyle Crescent Lane, Edinburgh, EH12 9EG
Website: http://heritagearchives.rbs.com/use-our-archives/visit-our-
archives.html
Email: archives@rbs.co.uk

Salford Diocesan Archives (Roman Catholic)

Contact the archivist Friar David Lannon to consult the collection.
St Augustine's Presbytery, Grosvenor Square, All Saints, Manchester,
M15 6BW
Website: http://www.salforddiocese.net/#!archives/cya8
Email: davelannon@aol.com
Tel: 0161 236 6762

Salford City Archives
The archives are accessed via SLHL (below). Archive catalogues are available at SLHL, and collection level descriptions are on GMLives.
Salford City Archives, Salford Museum and Art Gallery, Peel Park, The Crescent, Salford, M5 4WU
Website:www.salfordcommunityleisure.co.uk/culture/locations/salford -local-history-library
Email, archive: local.history@scll.co.uk
Tel, archives: 0161 778 0814

Salford Community Libraries
Locations of Salford libraries: www.salfordcommunityleisure.co.uk/ libraries/locations.
Website: www.salfordcommunityleisure.co.uk/libraries

Salford Local History Library
Genealogical sources: www.salford.gov.uk/births-marriages-and-deaths/family-history/genealogical-sources/; Salford Museum collections database: http://salfordmuseum.salford.gov.uk/.
Salford Local History Library, Peel Park, The Crescent, Salford, M5 4WU
Website: www.salfordcommunityleisure.co.uk/culture/salford-museum-and-art-gallery/local-history
Email: local.history@scll.co.uk
Tel: 0161 778 0814

Tameside Local Studies and Archives
Manchester Regiment Image Archive: www.manchester-regiment. org.uk/index.php; guide to family history materials: www. tameside. gov.uk/ familyhistory/archives/material; Guide to Absent Voters' Lists: www. tameside.gov.uk/archives/absentvoters; search Tameside burial records: http://web.tameside.gov.uk/RACAS.
Tameside Local Studies and Archives Centre, Central Library, Old Street, Ashton-under-Lyne, OL6 7SG
Website: www.tameside.gov.uk/archives
Tel: 0161 342 4242

Trafford Local Studies Centre
Sale Library, Sale Waterside, Sale, M33 7ZF

Website: www.trafford.gov.uk/residents/leisure-and-lifestyle/libraries/
archives-and-local-history.aspx
Email: trafflocals@trafford.gov.uk
Tel: 0161 912 3013

Waterways Archive, Ellesmere Port

The Waterways Archive, National Waterways Museum, South Pier
Road, Ellesmere Port, Cheshire, CH65 4FW
Website: http://collections.canalrivertrust.org.uk/home
Email: archives@canalrivertrust.org.uk
Tel: 0151 373 4378

Working Class Movement Library

Library reading room open by appointment only.
Working Class Movement Library, 51 The Crescent, Salford, M5 4WX
Website: www.wcml.org.uk
Tel: 0161 736 3601

UNIVERSITY LIBRARIES
University of Central Lancashire

Special Collections, The Library, University of Central Lancashire,
Preston, PR1 2HE
Website: https://www.uclan.ac.uk/students/study/ library/using_special_
collections.php
Email: LISCollections@uclan.ac.uk
Tel: 0177 289 2123

University of London, Senate House Library

Malet Street, London, WC1E 7HU
Website: www.senatehouselibrary.ac.uk
Email: shl.specialcollections@london.ac.uk
Tel: 0207 862 8470

University of Manchester Archives and Records Centre

Members of the public must register as a reader and make an
appointment to consult the collections. Online catalogue (ELGAR):
http://archives.li.man.ac.uk/ead/.
University Library, Burlington Street, Manchester, M15 6HQ

Website: www.library.manchester.ac.uk/search-resources/guide-to-special-collections/uomarchives/
Email: james.peters@manchester.ac.uk
Tel: 0161 275 5306

John Rylands Library, University of Manchester
A–Z list of Special Collections: www.library.manchester.ac.uk/search-resources/guide-to-special-collections/atoz/; guide to Methodist collections: www.library.manchester.ac.uk/media/services/library/deansgate/methodist-guide/Guide-to-Methodist-Resources-at-The-University-of-Manchester.pdf; online catalogue (ELGAR): http://archives.li.man.ac.uk/ead/; printed book catalogue: www.library.manchester.ac.uk/search-resources/books/.
The John Rylands Library, 150 Deansgate, Manchester, M3 3EH
Website: www.library.manchester.ac.uk/rylands/
Tel: 0161 275 3764
Email, Special Collections: uml.special-collections@manchester.ac.uk
Tel, Special Collections: 0161 275 3764
Email, Methodist archive: peter.nockles@manchester.ac.uk
Tel, Methodist archive: 0161 275 3755

Manchester Metropolitan University
The university's special collections include book illustration and textile design, the Manchester Society of Architects' Library and the North West Film Archive (see separate listing). Free admission to the reading room; contact the archivist in advance.
Special Collections, Sir Kenneth Green Library, All Saints, Manchester, M15 6BH
Website: www.specialcollections.mmu.ac.uk/collections.php
Email: lib-spec-coll@mmu.ac.uk
Tel: 0161 247 6107

University of Salford Archives and Special Collections
Visits by appointment only. To arrange a visit, or for archive queries, email Ian Johnston.
Clifford Whitworth Library, The Library, The University of Salford, The Crescent, Salford, M5 4WT
Website: www.salford.ac.uk/library/archives-and-special-collections

Email, archive: I.Johnston@salford.ac.uk
Tel, archive: 0161 295 6650

Modern Records Centre, University of Warwick

Business history sources:
www2.warwick.ac.uk/services/library/mrc/explorefurther/subject_guid
es/business; family history guide:
www2.warwick.ac.uk/services/library/mrc/explorefurther/subject_guid
es/family_history; occupational guide to trade unions:
www2.warwick.ac.uk/services/library/mrc/explorefurther/subject_guid
es/family_history/occupationalguide.pdf.
Modern Records Centre, University Library, University of Warwick
Coventry, CV4 7AL
Website:
www2.warwick.ac.uk/services/library/mrc/holdings/main_archives
Email: archives@warwick.ac.uk
Tel: 0247 652 4219

Appendix 2

USEFUL ADDRESSES

Duchy of Lancaster Office
The Duchy reserves the right to make a time charge for enquiries requiring research into Duchy records,
www.duchyoflancaster.com/about-the-duchy/records-charters.
The Duchy of Lancaster, 1 Lancaster Place, Strand, London, WC2E 7ED
Website: www.duchyoflancaster.com
Email: info@duchyoflancaster.co.uk

Duchy of Lancaster Solicitor's Office
The Duchy Solicitor administers the assets of people who die intestate (without a will) in Lancashire and Greater Manchester. To discover if the Duchy is dealing with the estate of a relative who died intestate (only within the county palatine), you must write to the Duchy Solicitor with a simple family tree showing your relationship to the deceased.
Solicitor for the Affairs of the Duchy of Lancaster, Farrer & Co.,
66 Lincoln's Inn Fields, London, WC2A 3LH
Website: www.farrer.co.uk
Tel: 0207 242 2022

General Register Office (England and Wales)
General Register Office Certificate Services Section, General Register Office
PO Box 2, Southport, PR8 2JD
Website: www.gro.gov.uk/gro/content/certificates/default.asp
Email: certificate.services@gro.gsi.gov.uk
Tel: 0300 123 1837

Leeds District Probate Registry

The Postal Searches and Copies Department, Leeds District Probate Registry, York House, York Place, Leeds, LS1 2BA; Find a Will: https://courttribunalfinder.service.gov.uk/courts/leeds-district-probate-registry
Email: LeedsDPRenquiries@hmcts.gsi.gov.uk
Tel: 0113 389 6133

Manchester District Probate Registry

Manchester District Probate Registry, Manchester Civil Justice Centre, Ground Floor, 1 Bridge Street West, PO Box 4240, Manchester, M60 1WJ
Website: https://courttribunalfinder.service.gov.uk/courts/manchester-district-probate-registry
Email: ManchesterDPRenquiries@hmcts.gsi.gov.uk
Tel, enquiries: 0161 240 5701
Tel, probate: 0300 123 1072

Manchester Registration Service

The Register Office, Heron House, 47 Lloyd Street, Manchester, M2 5LE
Website:www.manchester.gov.uk/info/500203/births_marriages_deaths_and_nationality/1144/buy_a_copy_certificate
Email: registeroffice@manchester.gov.uk
Tel: 0161 234 5005

Salford Register Office

Salford Civic Centre, Chorley Road, Swinton, Salford, M27 5DA
Website: www.salford.gov.uk/bmd.htm
Online enquiry form: http://bit.ly/2fjEX8j
Tel: 0161 909 6501

Principal Registry of the Family Division (Probate Service)

Website: https://www.gov.uk/wills-probate-inheritance

FAMILY HISTORY, HERITAGE AND HISTORY SOCIETIES

Catholic Record Society
The society is devoted to the history of Roman Catholicism and cannot help with family history research.
Website: www.catholic-history.org.uk/index.php

Chetham Society
List of Chetham Society publications:
www.chethamsociety.org.uk/publications.html
Website: www.chethamsociety.org.uk

Eccles and District History Society
The society holds regular meetings at Alexandra House, Liverpool Road, Peel Green, Eccles M30 7HB.
Website: http://edhs.btck.co.uk/
Email: eccleshistory@yahoo.co.uk

Federation of Family History Societies
The Federation of Family History Societies, PO Box 8857, Lutterworth, LE17 9BJ
Website: www.ffhs.org.uk
Email: info@ffhs.co.uk
Tel: 0800 085 6322

Guild of One-Name Studies
The Guild of One-Name Studies, Box G, 14 Charterhouse Buildings, Goswell Road, London, EC1M 7BA
Website: www.one-name.org

Email: guild@one-name.org
Tel: 0800 011 2182

Historic Society of Lancashire and Cheshire
The earlier volumes of the society's journals (up to 1999) have been
digitized and put on their website. Index of journals published:
http://bit.ly/zNXazK.
Membership: Dr J.E. Hollinshead, 28 Tewkesbury Close, Woolton,
Liverpool, L25 9RY
Website: www.hslc.org.uk
Email: info@hslc.org.uk

The Institute of Heraldic and Genealogical Studies
The Institute of Heraldic and Genealogical Studies, 79–82 Northgate,
Canterbury, Kent, CT1 1BA
Website: www.ihgs.ac.uk/
Email: enquiries@ihgs.ac.uk
Tel: 0122 776 8664

Lancashire and Cheshire Antiquarian Society
The Society's Library is housed at MCL. A member's library ticket,
available from the Honorary Secretary, is required to access the collection.
Mr M. Garratt, Honorary Membership Secretary, Lancashire and
Cheshire Antiquarian Society, 59 Malmesbury Road, Cheadle Hulme,
Cheadle, SK8 7QL
Website: www.landcas.org.uk
Email: morrisgarratt@sky.com

Lancashire and Cheshire Record Society Publications
Website: http://rslc.org.uk/publications/

Lancashire Local History Federation
Website: www.lancashirehistory.org/membersoci.htm

Lancashire Family History and Heraldry Society
Lancashire Family History and Heraldry Society, 2 Straits,
Oswaldtwistle, Lancashire, BB5 3LU
Website: www.lfhhs.org/home.php

Email: sales@lfhhs.org
Tel: 0125 423 9919

Lancashire Parish Register Society

Alphabetical list of parish registers published by the society: www.
lprs.org.uk/publications/.
Treasurer and Membership Secretary, Mrs Jackie Roberts, Lancashire
Parish Register Society, 13 Corrie Drive, Kearsley, Bolton, BL4 8RG
Website: www.lprs.org.uk

Manchester & Lancashire Family History Society

The MLFHS has three branches: Bolton and District, Oldham and
District, and Anglo-Scottish Ancestry FHS. The society has a Help
Desk in MCL, open Mon–Fri, except Bank Holidays, 10.30am–3.30pm.
Manchester & Lancashire FHS, 3rd Floor, Manchester Central
Library, St Peter's Square, Manchester, M2 5PD
Website: www.mlfhs.org.uk
Email enquiry form: www.mlfhs.org.uk/contact/email.php
Tel: 0161 234 1060

Manchester Region Industrial Archaeological Society

Manchester Metropolitan University Business School,
Seminar Room 301, All Saints Campus, Oxford Road, Manchester,
M15 6BH
Website: www.mrias.co.uk/
Tel: 0161 247 2838

Manchester Victorian Society

Website: www.victoriansociety.org.uk/manchester/

North West Catholic History Society

Membership: Brian Farrimond, The Treasurer, 11 Tower Hill,
Ormskirk, Lancashire, L39 2EE
Website: www.nwcatholichistory.org.uk/

North West Group of Family History Societies

Website: www.nwgfhs.org.uk

Salford Local History Society
The society holds regular meetings in the Audio-Visual Room of
Salford Museum and Art Gallery.
Website: http://slhs.btck.co.uk/
Email: roy.bullock@ntlworld.com

Society of Genealogists
National Library and Education Centre for Family History:
www.sog.org.uk/the-library.
Society of Genealogists, 14 Charterhouse Buildings, Goswell Road,
London, EC1M 7BA
Website: www.societyofgenealogists.com
Email: membership@sog.org.uk
Tel: 0207 251 8799

Appendix 4

USEFUL WEBSITES

Ashton Pals
Website dedicated to the Ashton Territorials, 9th Battalion of the
Manchester Regiment: http://ashtonpals.webs.com

Blackley 1891 Census Transcripts
Includes Manchester and Salford Reformatory for Boys.
www.blackley1891.co.uk/

Cemetery Records Online (Lancashire)
http://interment.net/uk/eng/lancashire.htm

FamilySearch Wiki, Manchester
https://familysearch.org/learn/wiki/en/Manchester

GENUKI Manchester
www.genuki.org.uk/big/eng/LAN/Manchester/

GENUKI Salford
www.genuki.org.uk/big/eng/LAN/Salford/

Greater Manchester Churches Preservation Society
www.manchesterchurches.btck.co.uk/

Little Hulton History
http://hultonhistory.btck.co.uk/

The Long, Long Trail
A comprehensive First World War website: www.1914-
1918.net/index.html

Help on how to find soldiers' records: www.1914 1918.net/records.html
Lancashire Fusiliers: www.1914-1918.net/lancsfus.htm
Manchester Regiment: http://www.1914-1918.net/mancs.htm

Manchester Association for Masonic Research (MAMR)

The association covers freemasonry for East and West Lancashire, and Cheshire. www.pglel.co.uk/MAMR/MAMR.asp

Manchester Bolton and Bury Canal Society

www.mbbcs.org.uk/

Manchester Historical Maps (beta)

http://manchester.publicprofiler.org/beta

Our Manchester

Eight historical websites linked to the Manchester area: http://manchesterhistory.net/manchester/ManMenu.html

Manchester's Radical History

Blog with articles exploring the city's Radical past: https://radical manchester.wordpress.com/

Manchester Regiment Group

www.themanchesters.org

Manchester Regiments Group Forum

www.themanchesters.org/forum/index.php

Mancuniensis

Historical and genealogical information for Salford Hundred: www.mancuniensis.info/

NorthWest Labour History Society

www.nwlh.org.uk/

Police Station History in Victorian Manchester

www.victorianpolicestations.org/

Pubs of Manchester Past and Present
History of pubs in and out of the city centre: http://pubs-of-manchester.blogspot.co.uk/

Quaker FHS: Researching in Lancashire
www.rootsweb.ancestry.com/~engqfhs/Research/counties/lancs.htm

Rootsweb
Online mailing list for Manchester and Salford family history. Search the message archive by name or subject: http://lists.rootsweb.ancestry.com/index/intl/ENG/ENG-MANCHESTER.html

Old Postcards (Manchester and Salford)
www.manchesterpostcards.com/

Old Street Maps, Manchester, 1772–2010
http://splintmap.geog.ucl.ac.uk/~ollie/manchester/

Salford History Blog
http://salfordhistory.blogspot.co.uk/
List of Salford newspapers published and name changes:
http://salfordhistory.blogspot.co.uk/2014/08/salford-newspapers.html

Salford Streets Museum
Online image archive with A–Z of lost Salford streets: www.streetsmuseum.co.uk/Streets_Museum/Streetsmuseum.html

Salford War Memorials Forum
http://salfordwarmemorials.proboards.com/

Waterways in Manchester and Salford
www.penninewaterways.co.uk/manchester/index.htm

MISCELLANEOUS GENEALOGY WEBSITES
Curious Fox www.curiousfox.com/
Cyndi's List www.cyndislist.com/uk
Deceased Online https://www.deceasedonline.com/
Family Relatives www.familyrelatives.com

Free Reg www.freereg.org.uk
Free UK Census www.freecen.org.uk
Irish Genealogy www.irishgenealogy.ie
Lost Cousins www.lostcousins.com/
National Archives of Ireland www.nationalarchives.ie
Public Record Office of Northern Ireland
https://www.nidirect.gov.uk/proni
Roots Chat www.rootschat.com
Roots Ireland www.rootsireland.ie
ScotlandsPeople www.scotlandspeople.gov.uk

Appendix 5

POOR LAW UNIONS IN MANCHESTER AND SALFORD

Chorlton Union (1837–96)
Ardwick, Barton-upon-Irwell (1841), Burnage, Chorlton-cum-Hardy, Chorlton-upon-Medlock, Didsbury, Flixton (1841), Gorton, Hulme, Levenshulme, Moss Side, Openshaw, Rusholme, Stretford, Urmston (1841), Withington. In 1894, Gorton was sub-divided into Gorton and West Gorton.

Salford Union (1838–1930)
Salford, Broughton, Pendleton and Pendlebury.

Manchester Union (1841–50)
Blackley, Bradford, Cheetham, Crumpsall, Failsworth, Harpurhey, Great and Little Heaton, Manchester, Moston, Newton and Prestwich. In April 1850 Manchester Township became a Poor Law Union in its own right and the remaining townships formed the new Prestwich Union.

Barton-upon Irwell Union (1849)
Barton-upon-Irwell, Flixton and Urmston were separated from the Chorlton Union to form the Barton-upon-Irwell Union. Clifton, Stretford and Worsley joined this new Union. A large part of the modern City of Salford was covered by this Union.

Prestwich Union (1850–1915)
Beswick (1858), Blackley, Bradford, Cheetham, Clayton (1894), Crumpsall, Failsworth, Harpurhey, Great and Little Heaton, Moston, Newton and Prestwich.

North Manchester Township (1896–1915)

All the constituents of Prestwich Union except Prestwich and Failsworth, i.e. Beswick, Blackley, Bradford, Cheetham, Clayton (1894), Crumpsall, Harpurhey, Great and Little Heaton, Moston and Newton.

South Manchester Township (1896–1915)

Chorlton-upon-Medlock, Ardwick, Hulme, Rusholme, Openshaw and West Gorton.

Manchester Union (1915)

Manchester Township, South Manchester Township and Prestwich Union merged to form the Manchester Union.

MCC Public Assistance Committee (1930)

The Manchester Board of Guardians was dissolved on 31 March 1930 and Manchester City Council's Public Assistance Committee took over its duties. This body was later renamed the Social Welfare Committee.

National Assistance (1948)

The end of the Poor Law. The National Assistance Board became responsible for the relief of the poor and destitute.

Appendix 6

TIMELINE OF KEY DATES

1230	The town of Salford receives its charter.
1301	The town of Manchester receives its charter.
1421	Manchester Collegiate Church is founded.
1573	Earliest surviving register for Manchester Collegiate Church.
1653	Chetham's Library and Hospital are founded.
1792	Manchester and Salford Police Commissioners Act.
1838	Manchester receives its charter of municipal incorporation.
1844	Salford receives its charter of municipal incorporation.
1853	Manchester becomes a city.
1889	Manchester and Salford each becomes a county borough.
1926	Salford becomes a city.
1974	Manchester and Salford become part of Greater Manchester County.
1986	Manchester City Council and Salford City Council become unitary authorities.

Appendix 7

PLACES TO VISIT

A selection of the many historic and heritage places of interest in Manchester and Salford.

Astley Green Colliery Museum
Lancashire's last surviving pit head gear and colliery engine house.
The Secretary, Astley Green Colliery Museum, Higher Green Lane,
Astley Green, Tyldesley, Manchester, M29 7JB
Website: www.agcm.org.uk
Email: info@agcm.org.uk

Elizabeth Gaskell's House
Home of the famous novelist.
84 Plymouth Grove, Manchester, M13 9LW
Website: www.elizabethgaskellhouse.co.uk/
Email: enquiries@elizabethgaskellhouse.co.uk
Tel: 0161 273 2215

Greater Manchester Transport Museum
Museum of Transport, Boyle Street, Cheetham, Manchester, M8 8UW
Website: www.gmts.co.uk/index.html
Email: email@gmts.co.uk
Tel: 0161 205 2122

Imperial War Museum North
The Quays, Trafford Wharf Road, Manchester, M17 1TZ
Website: www.iwm.org.uk/visits/iwm-north
Tel: 0161 836 4000

Lancashire Infantry Museum
The Curator, Lancashire Infantry Museum, Fulwood Barracks, Preston, PR2 8AA
Website: www.lancashireinfantrymuseum.org.uk
Email: enquiries@lancashireinfantrymuseum.org.uk
Tel: 0177 226 0584

The Lowry
Gallery and arts complex housing over 400 works by Salford artist L.S. Lowry. The archive at The Lowry comprises exhibition catalogues, L.S. Lowry correspondence, photos and press cuttings. Access to the archive is by appointment only; contact the curator, www.thelowry.com/ls-lowry/the-ls-lowry-archive.
Pier 8, Salford Quays, M50 3AZ
Website: www.thelowry.com/
Email, curator: claire.stewart@thelowry.com
Tel, curator: 0161 876 2096
Tel, box office: 0843 208 6000

Manchester City Football Club Museum
Etihad Stadium, Sportcity, Manchester, M11 3FF
Website: https://mancity.com/
Email: chris.nield@mcfc.co.uk
Tel: 0161 438 7820

Museum of the Manchester Regiment
Museum of the Manchester Regiment, Ashton Town Hall, Market Place, Ashton-under-Lyne, OL6 6DL
Website: www.tameside.gov.uk/museumsgalleries/mom
Tel: 0161 343 2878

Manchester United Museum
Manchester United Football Club, Sir Matt Busby Way, Old Trafford, Manchester, M16 0RA
Website: http://www.manutd.com/en/Visit-Old-Trafford/Museum-And-Stadium-Tour/Museum.aspx
Email: curator@manutd.co.uk
Tel: 0161 868 8000

Museum of Science and Industry, Manchester
Working mill engines and textile machinery demonstrations.
Collections Centre.
Museum of Science & Industry, Liverpool Road, Castlefield,
Manchester, M3 4FP
Website: http://msimanchester.org.uk/
Email, Collections Centre: collections@msimanchester.org.uk
Tel, Collection Centre: 0161 606 0127
Tel, museum: 0161 832 2244

National Football Museum
Explore 150 years of football heritage.
National Football Museum, Urbis Building, Cathedral Gardens,
Manchester, M4 3BG
Website: www.nationalfootballmuseum.com
Email: info@nationalfootballmuseum.com
Tel: 0161 605 8200

The Pankhurst Centre
60–2 Nelson Street, Chorlton-upon-Medlock, Manchester, M13 9WP
Website: www.thepankhurstcentre.org.uk
Email: admin@thepankhurstcentre.org.uk
Tel: 0161 273 5673

People's History Museum
Exhibitions on the history of Britain's workers. Major collection of
historic trade-union and political banners.
People's History Museum, Left Bank, Spinningfields, Manchester,
M3 3ER
Website: www.phm.org.uk
Email: info@phm.org.uk
Tel: 0161 838 9190

Platt Hall Gallery of Costume
Gallery of Costume, Platt Hall, Rusholme, Manchester, M14 5LL
Website: http://manchesterartgallery.org/visit/gallery-of-costume/
Tel: 0161 245 7245

Salford Lads' Club
The Club has an Archive Room with a collection of photos, records, film reels and memorabilia.
St Ignatius Walk, Salford, M5 3RX
Website: https://salfordladsclub.org.uk/
Email: info@salfordladsclub.org.uk
Tel: 0161 872 3767

INDEX